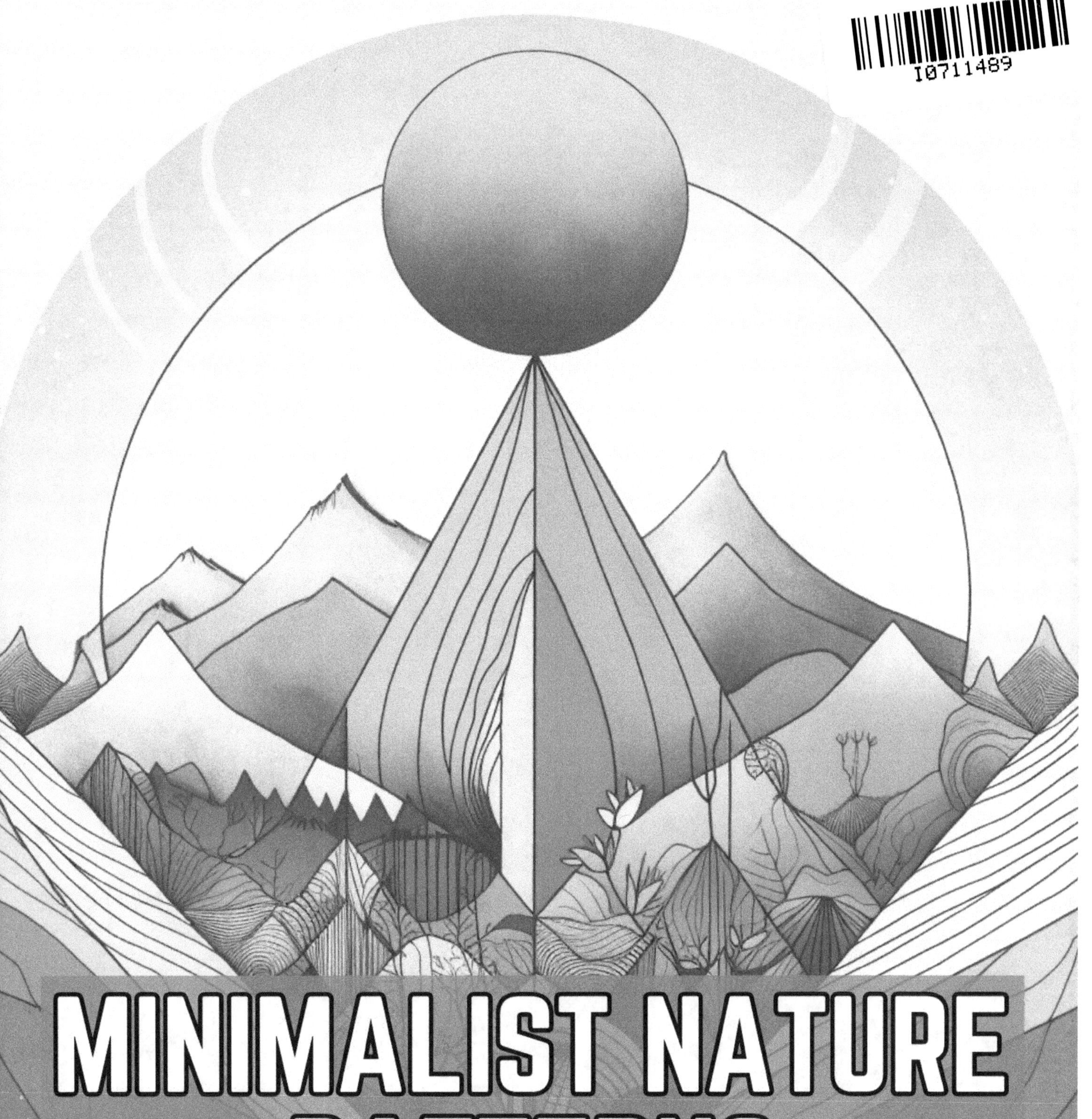

I0711489
MINIMALIST NATURE
PATTERNS
COLORING BOOK

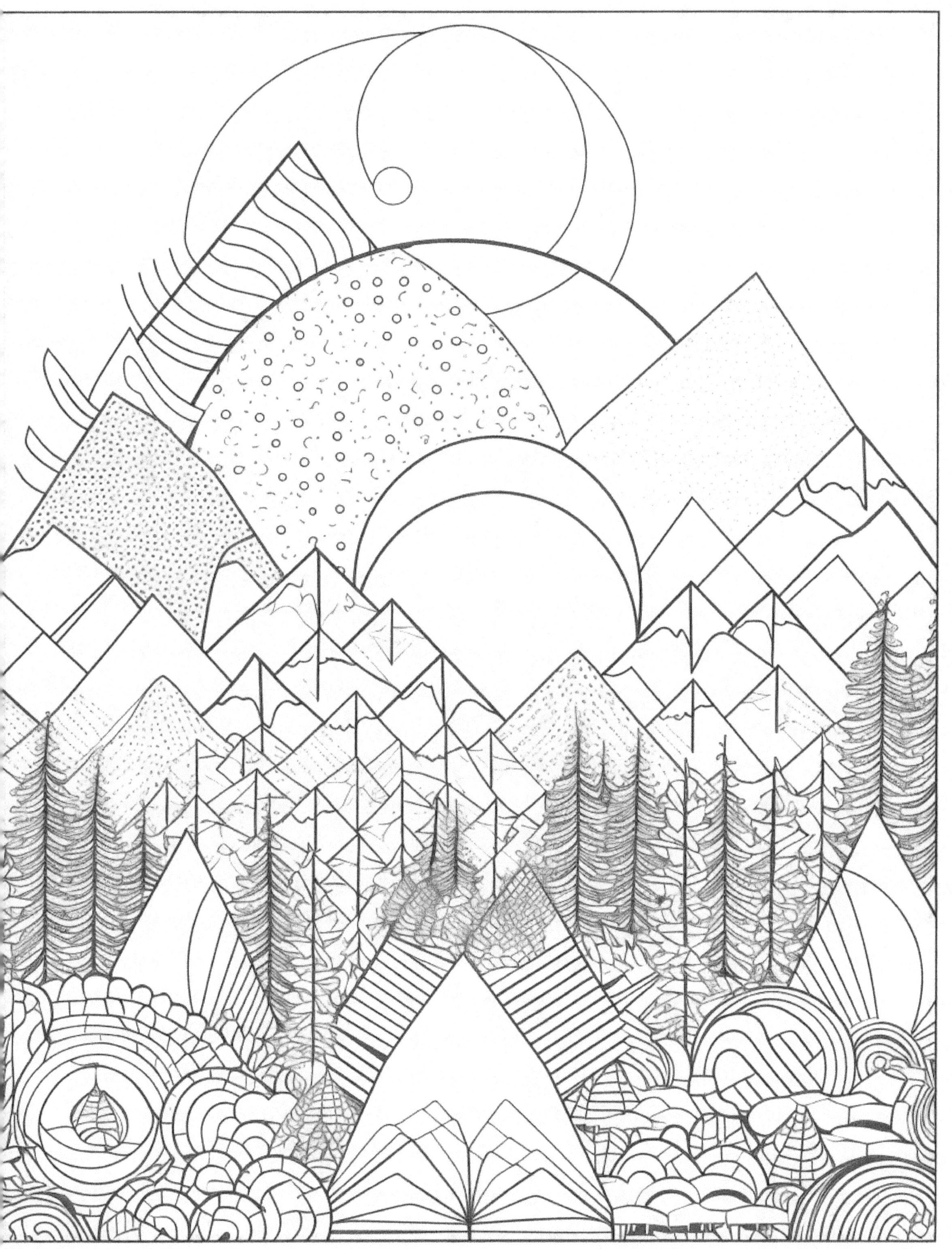

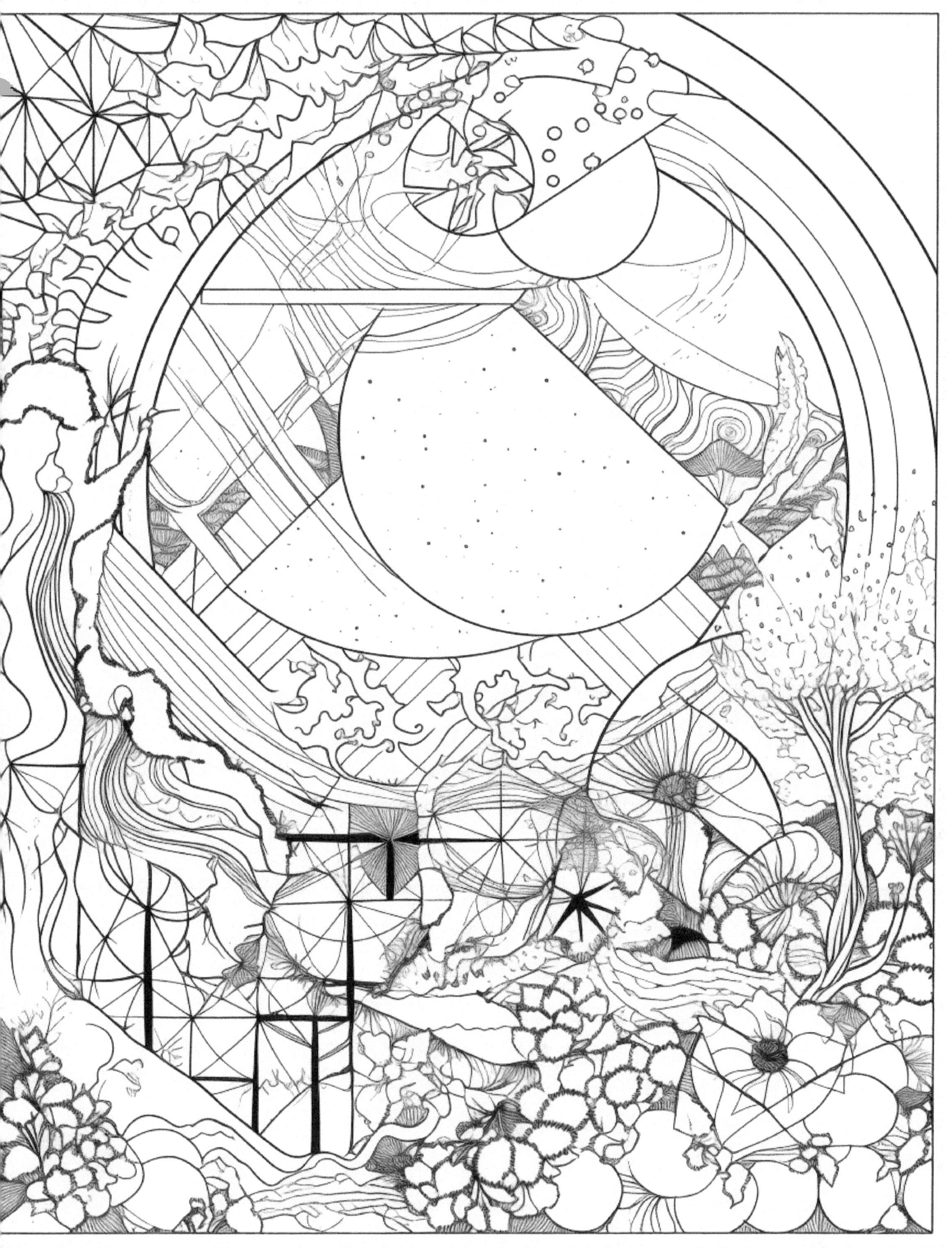

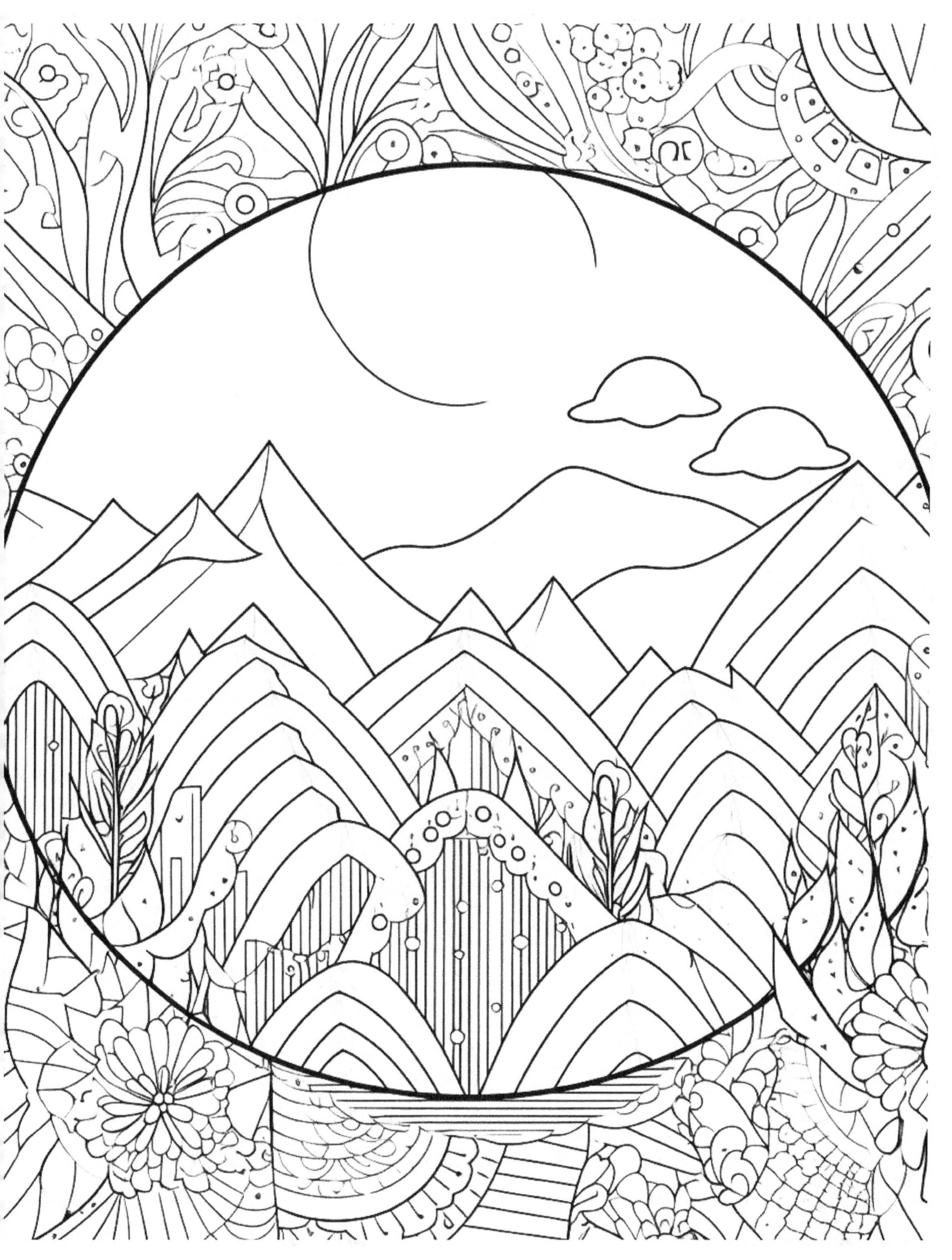

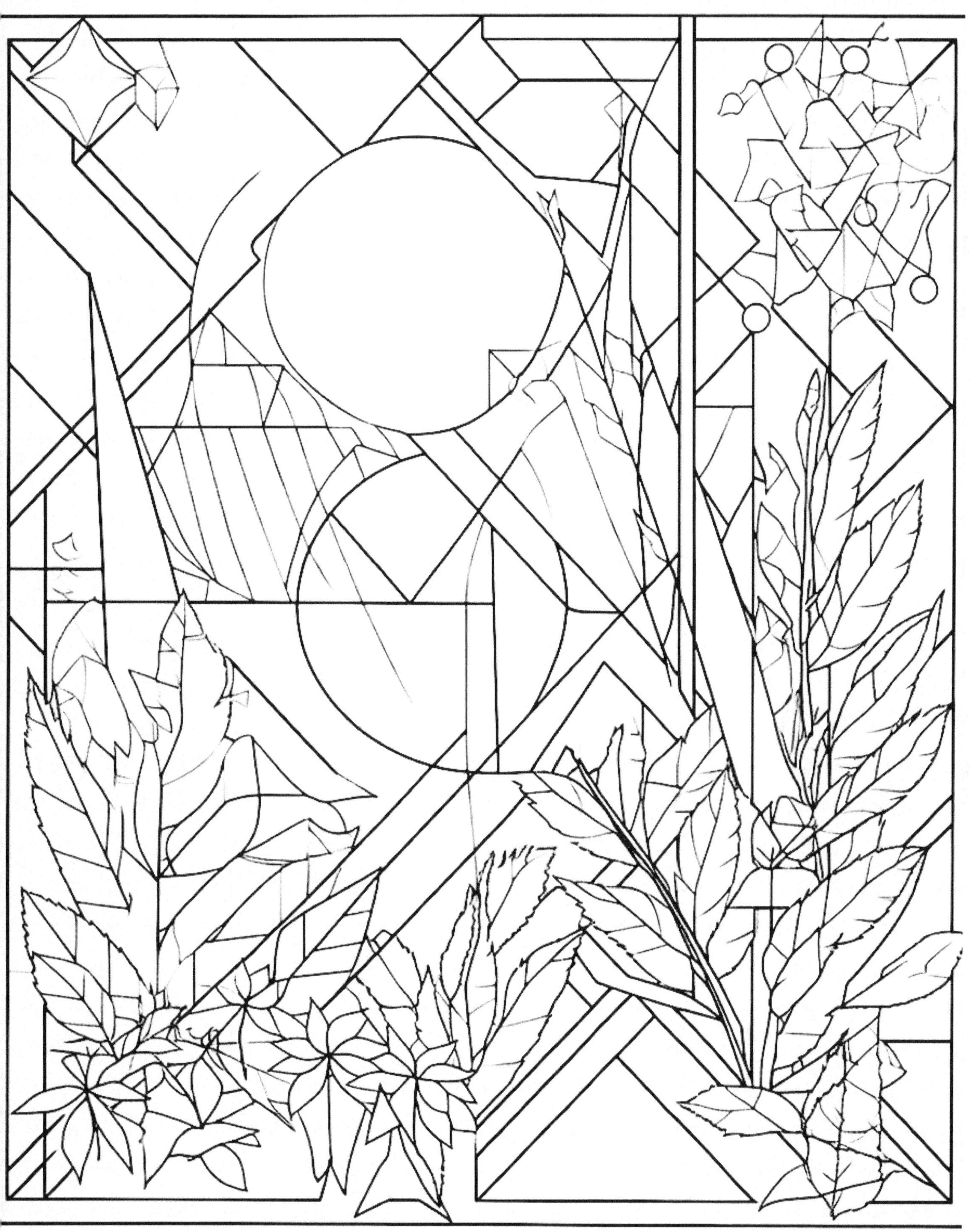

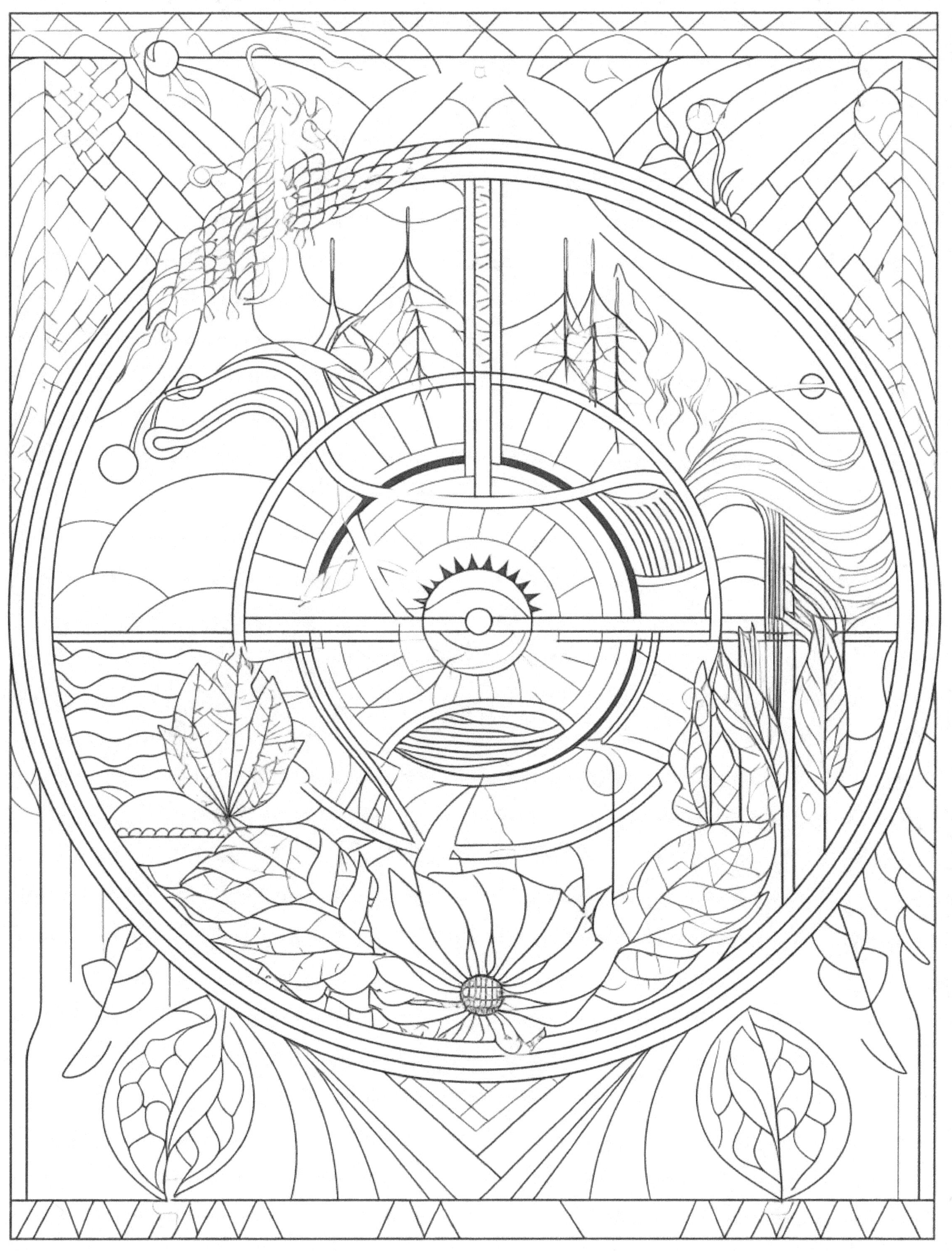

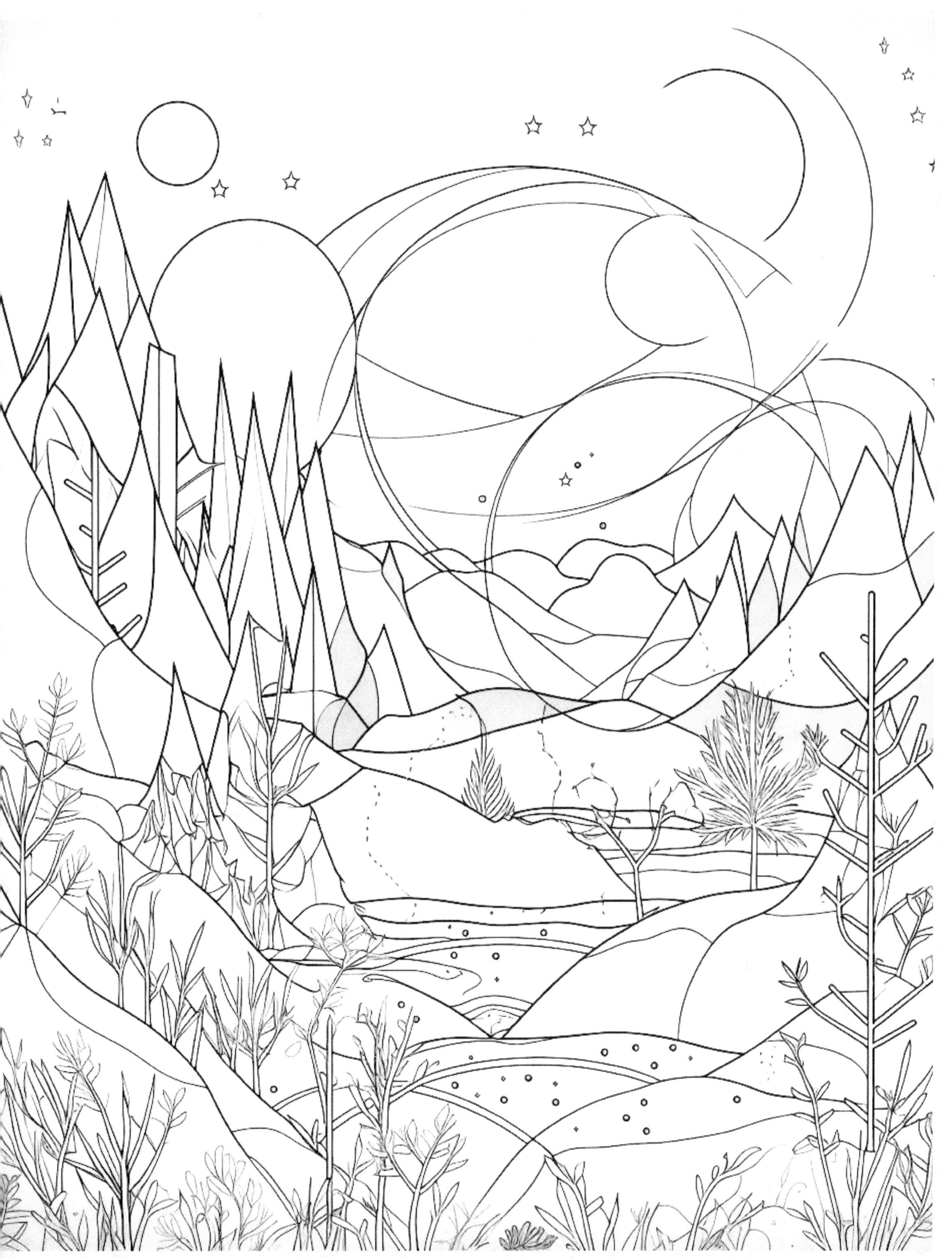

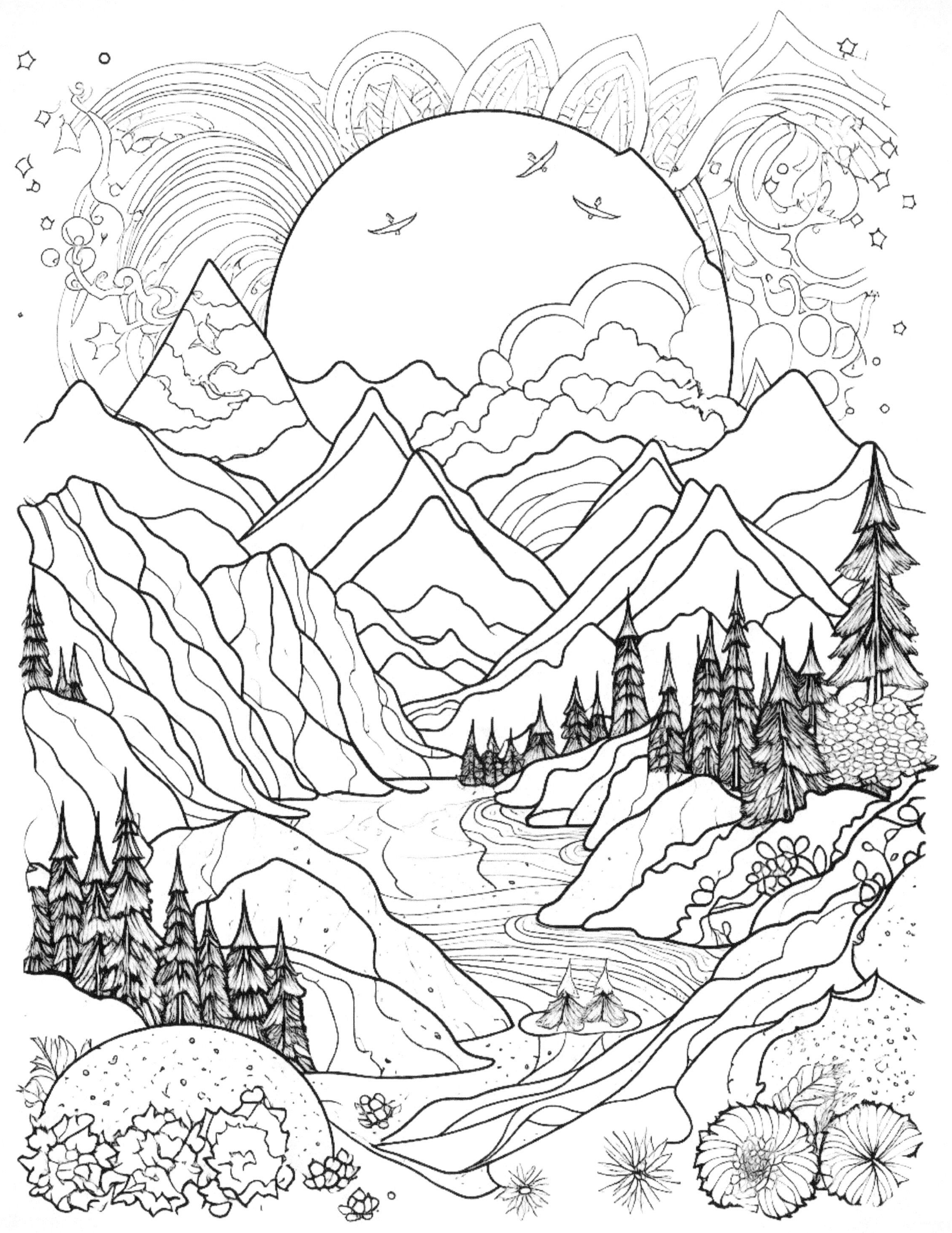

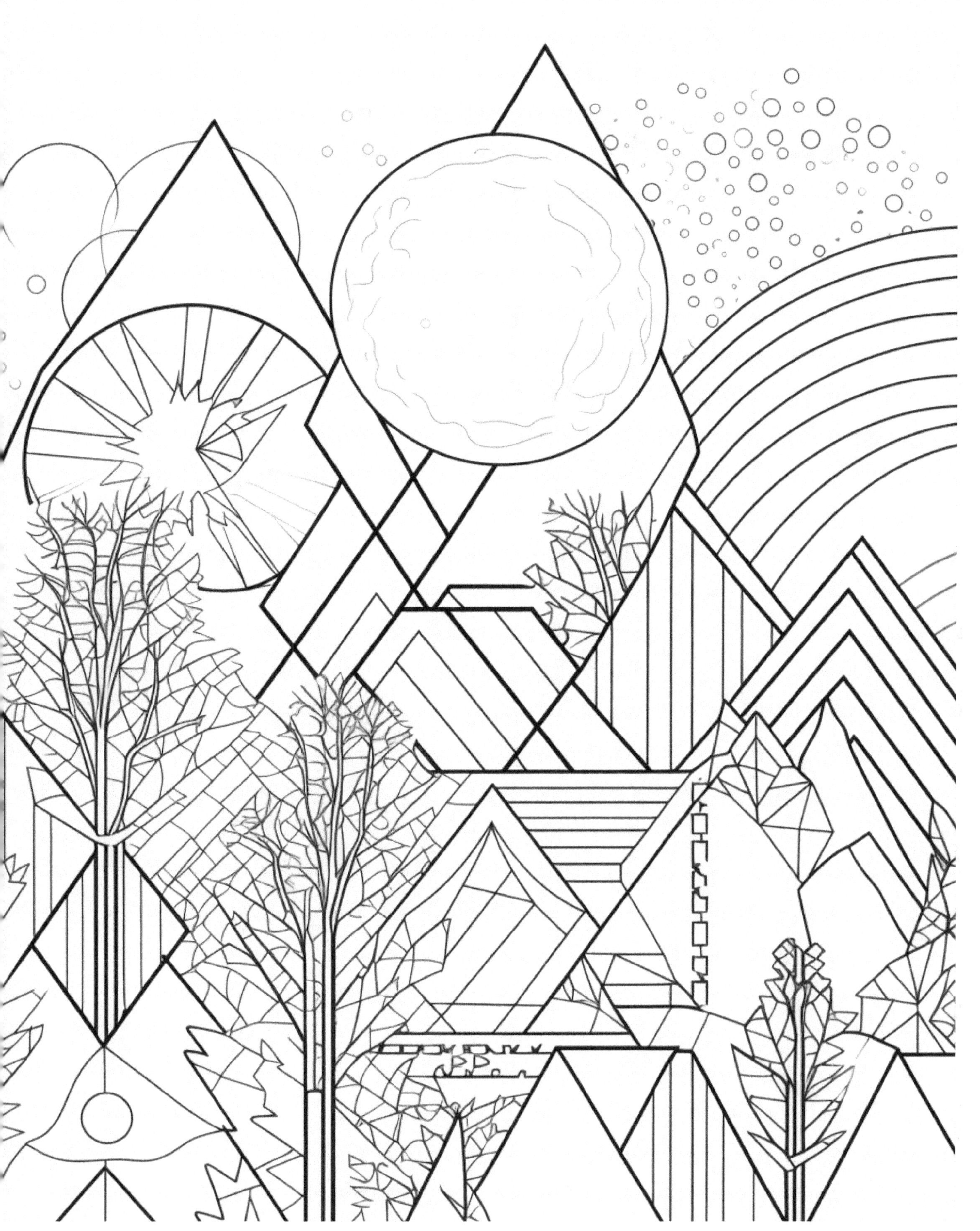

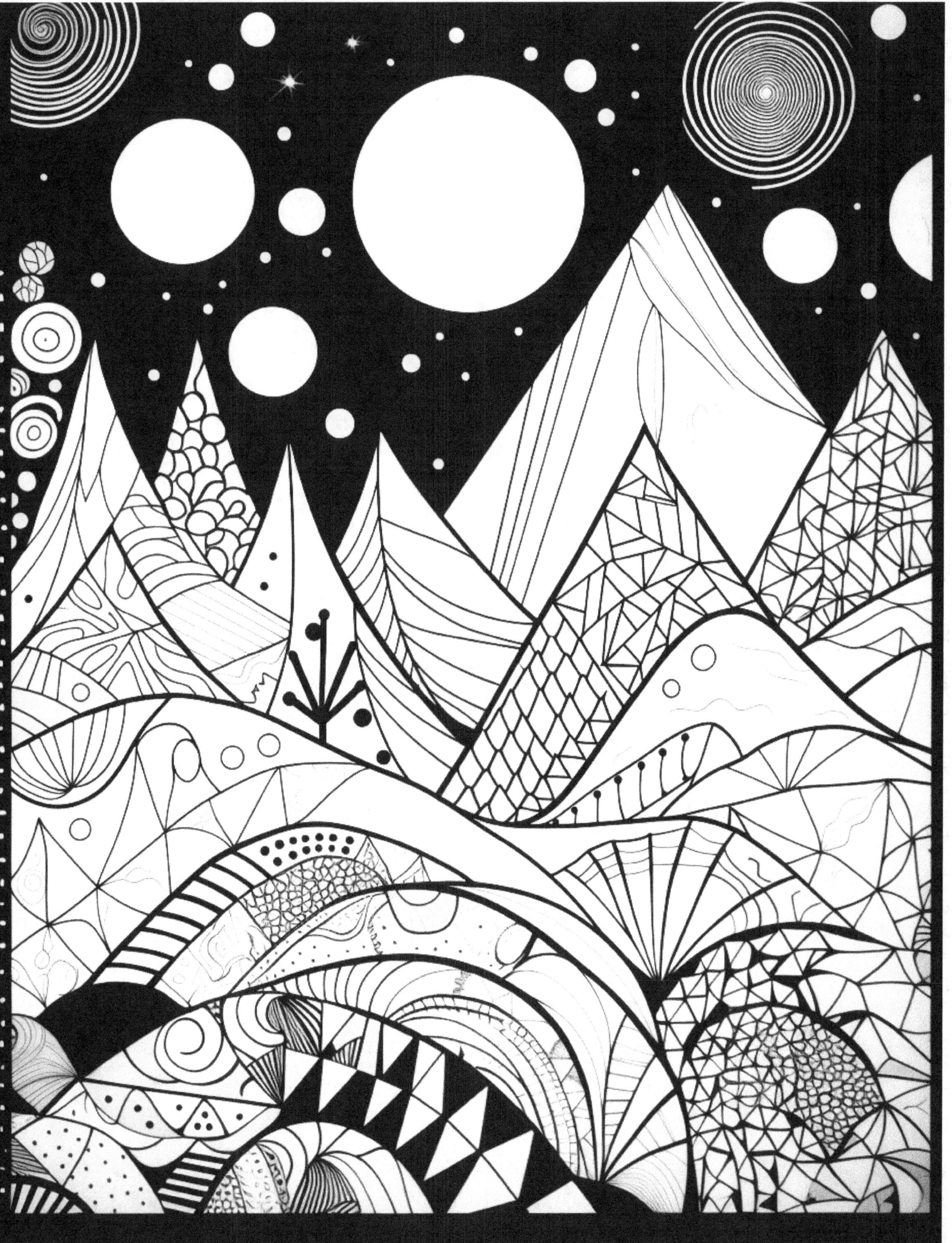

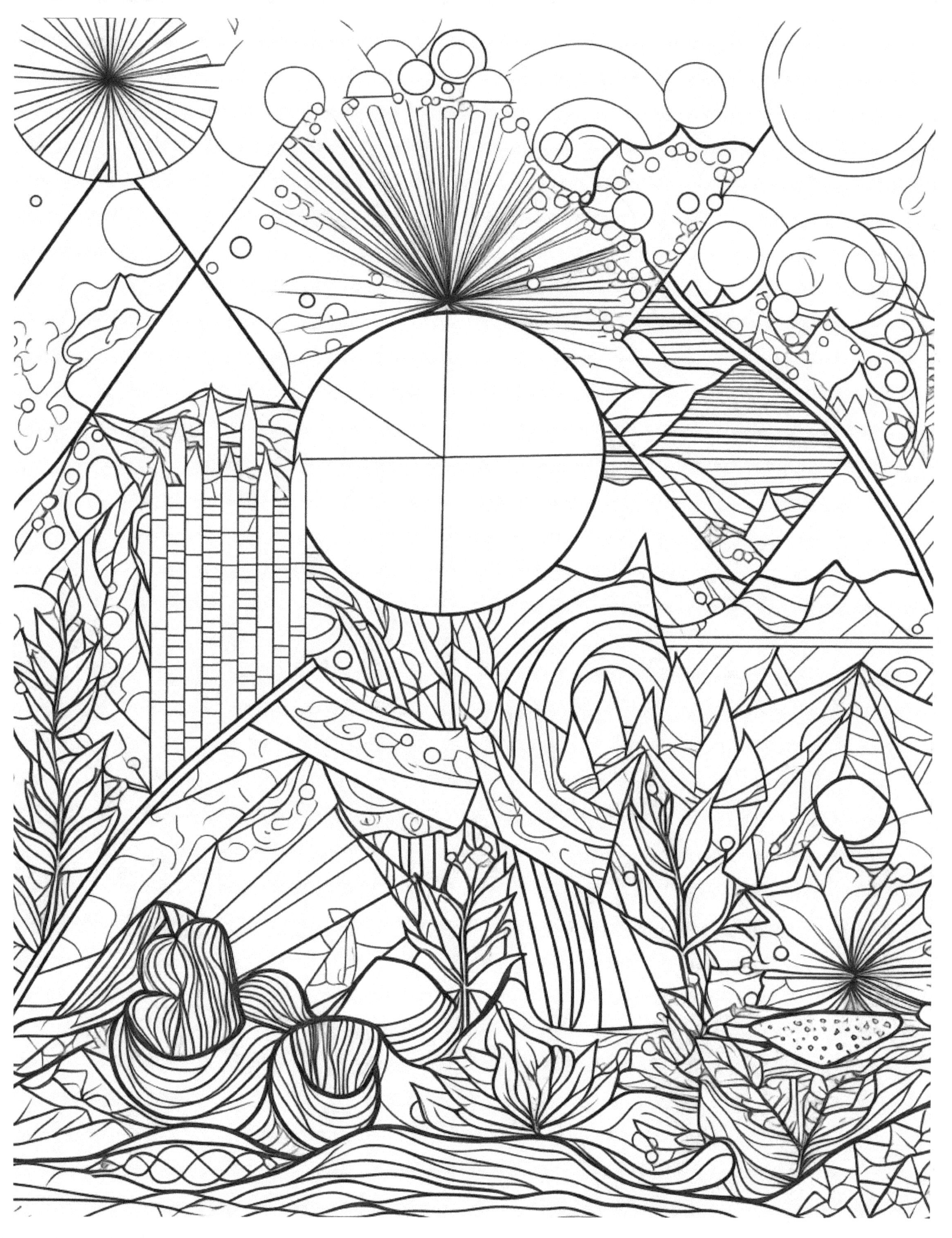

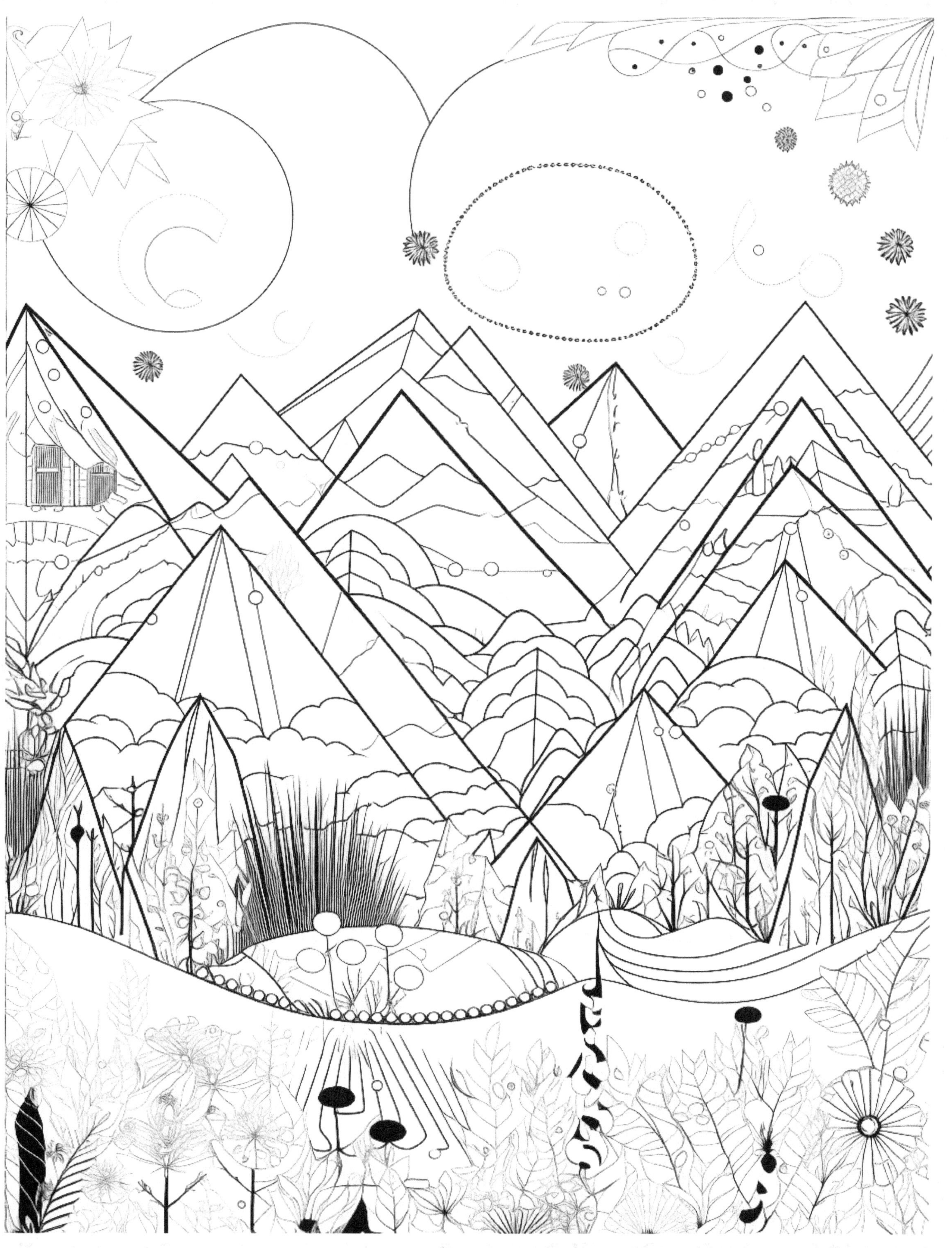

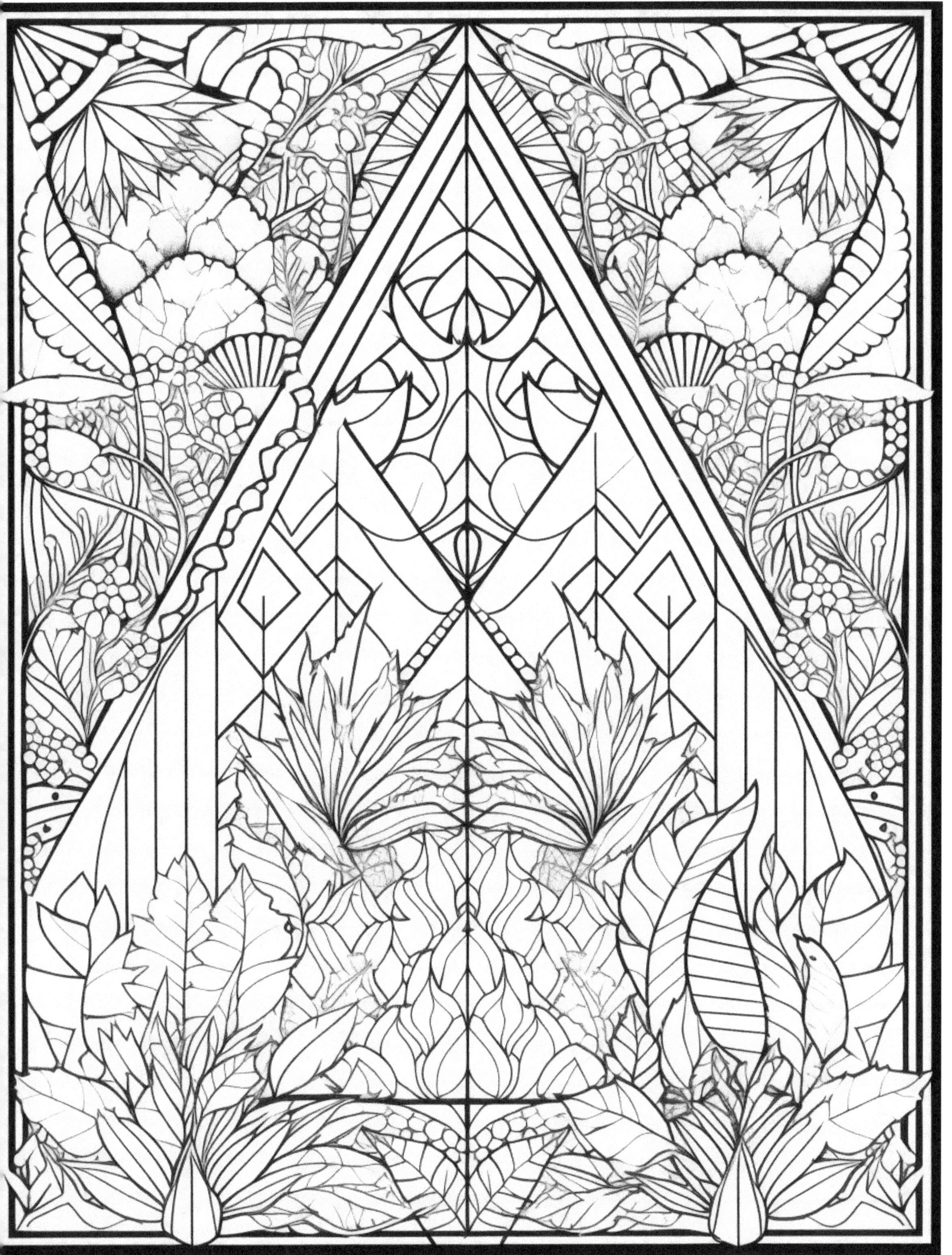

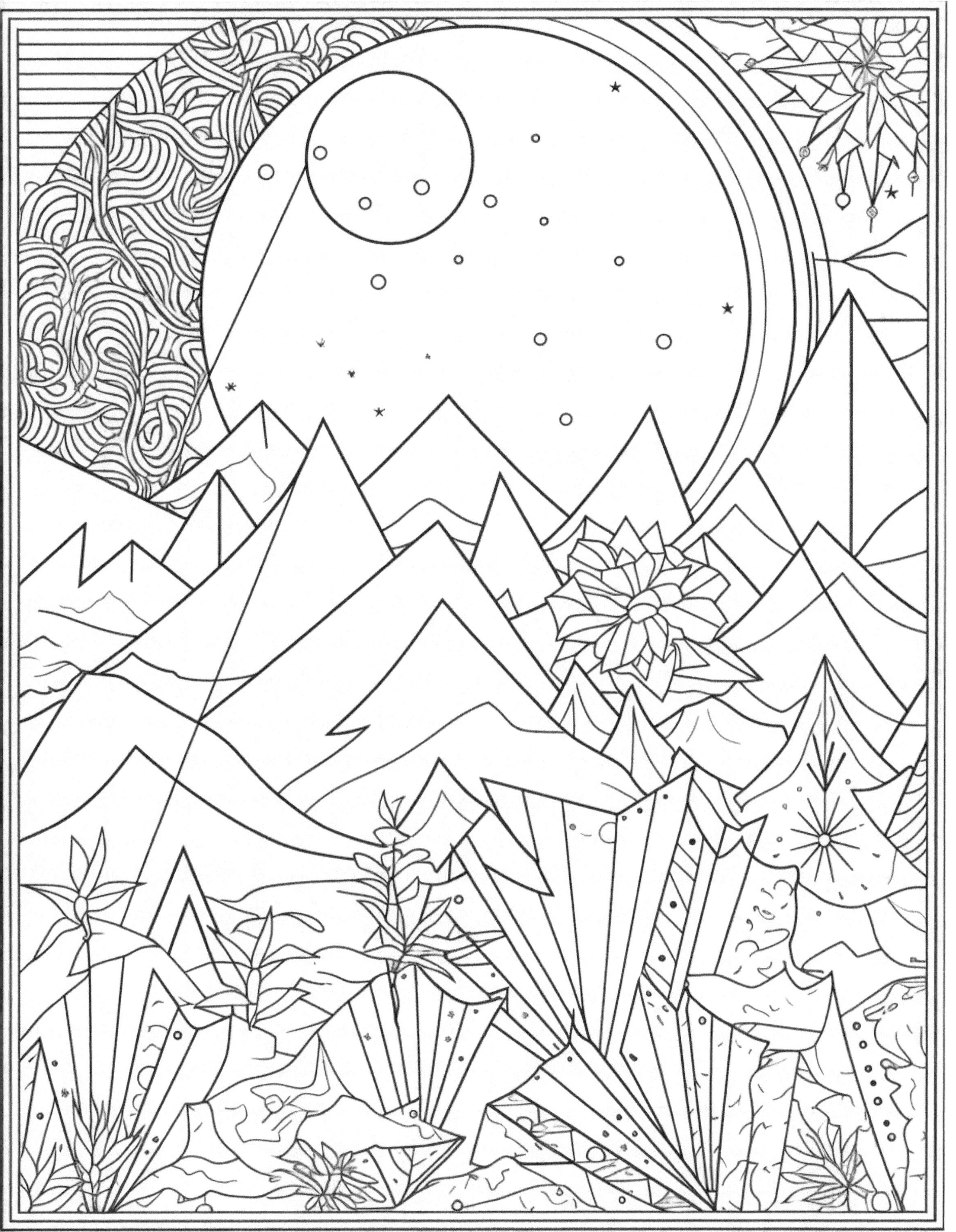

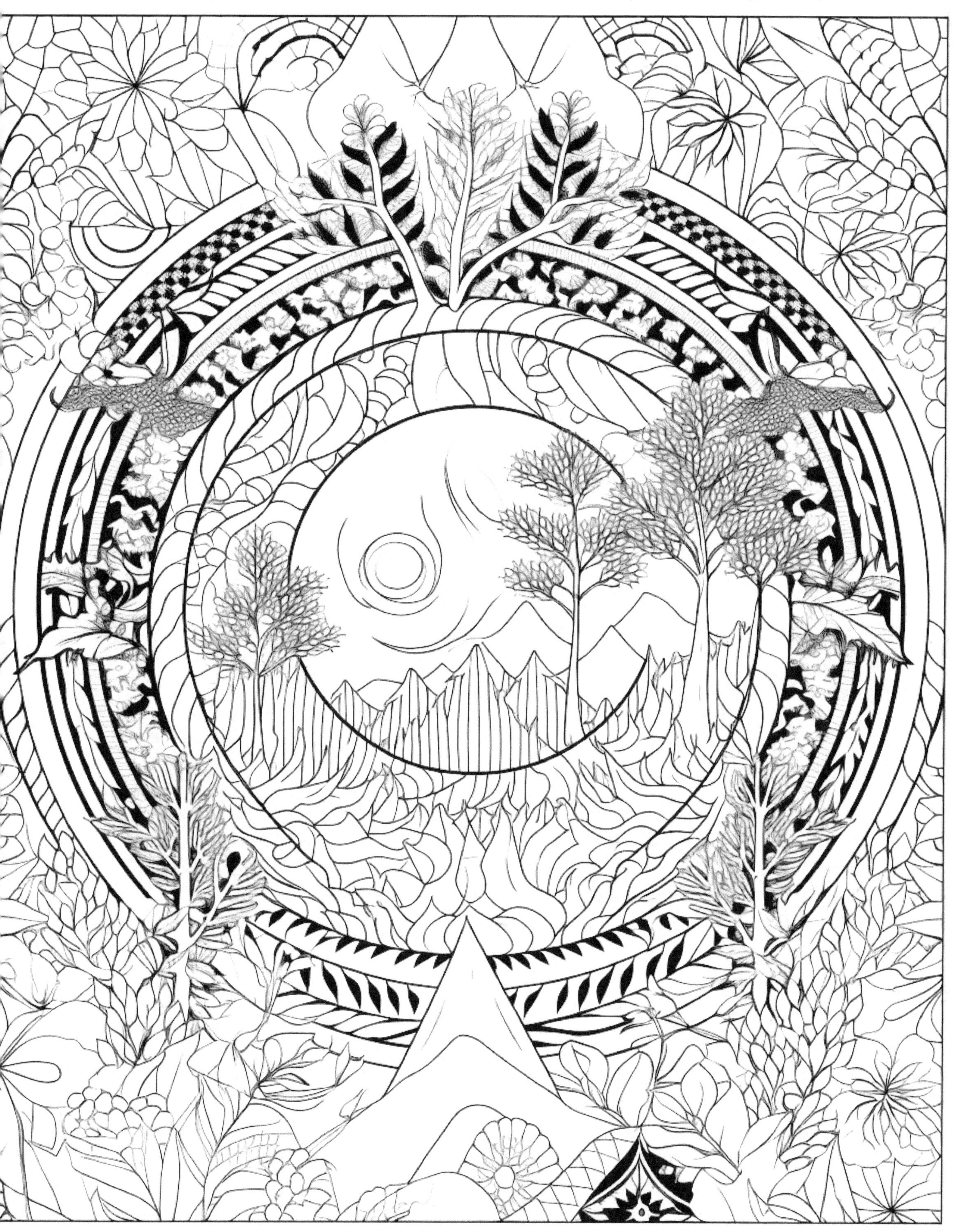

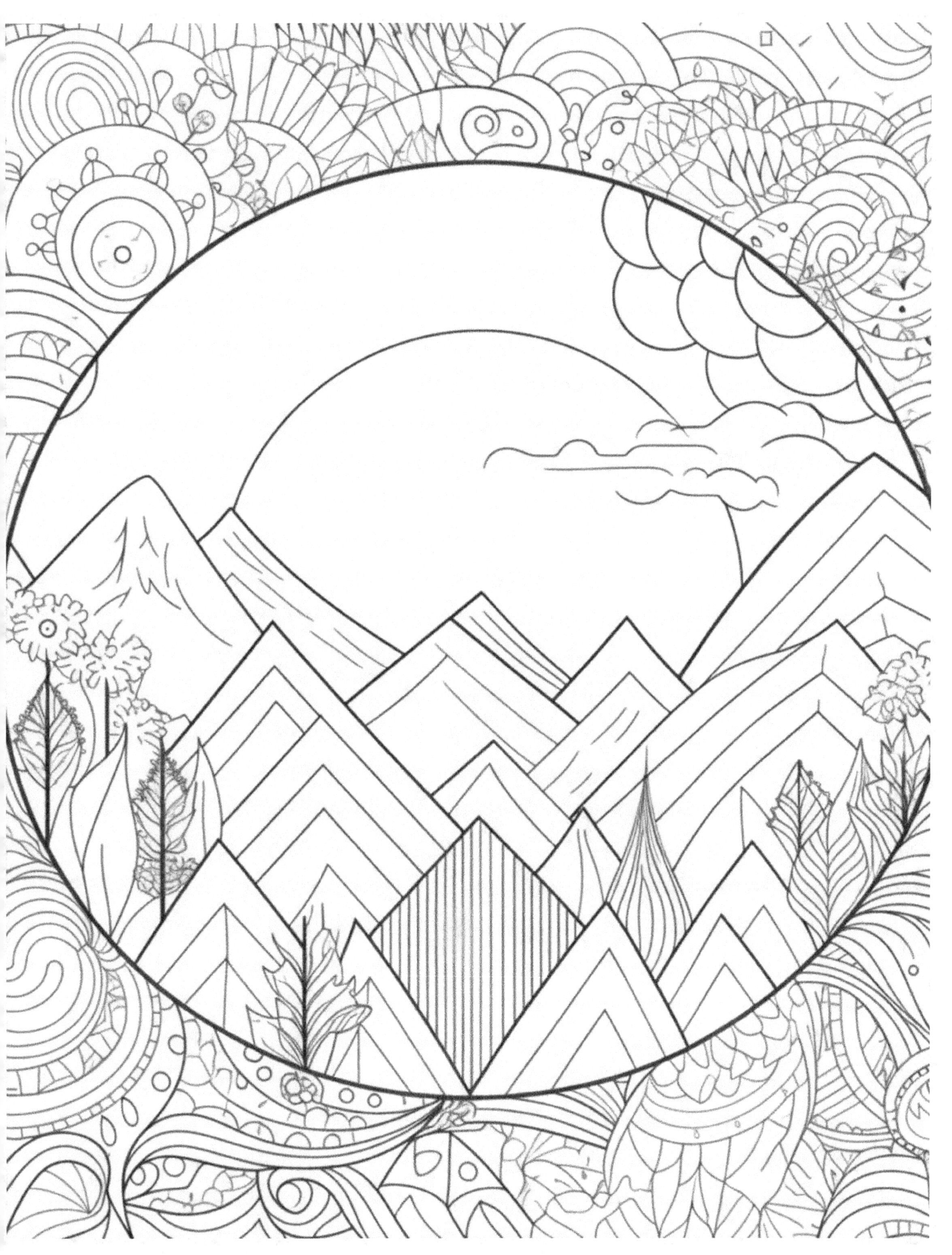

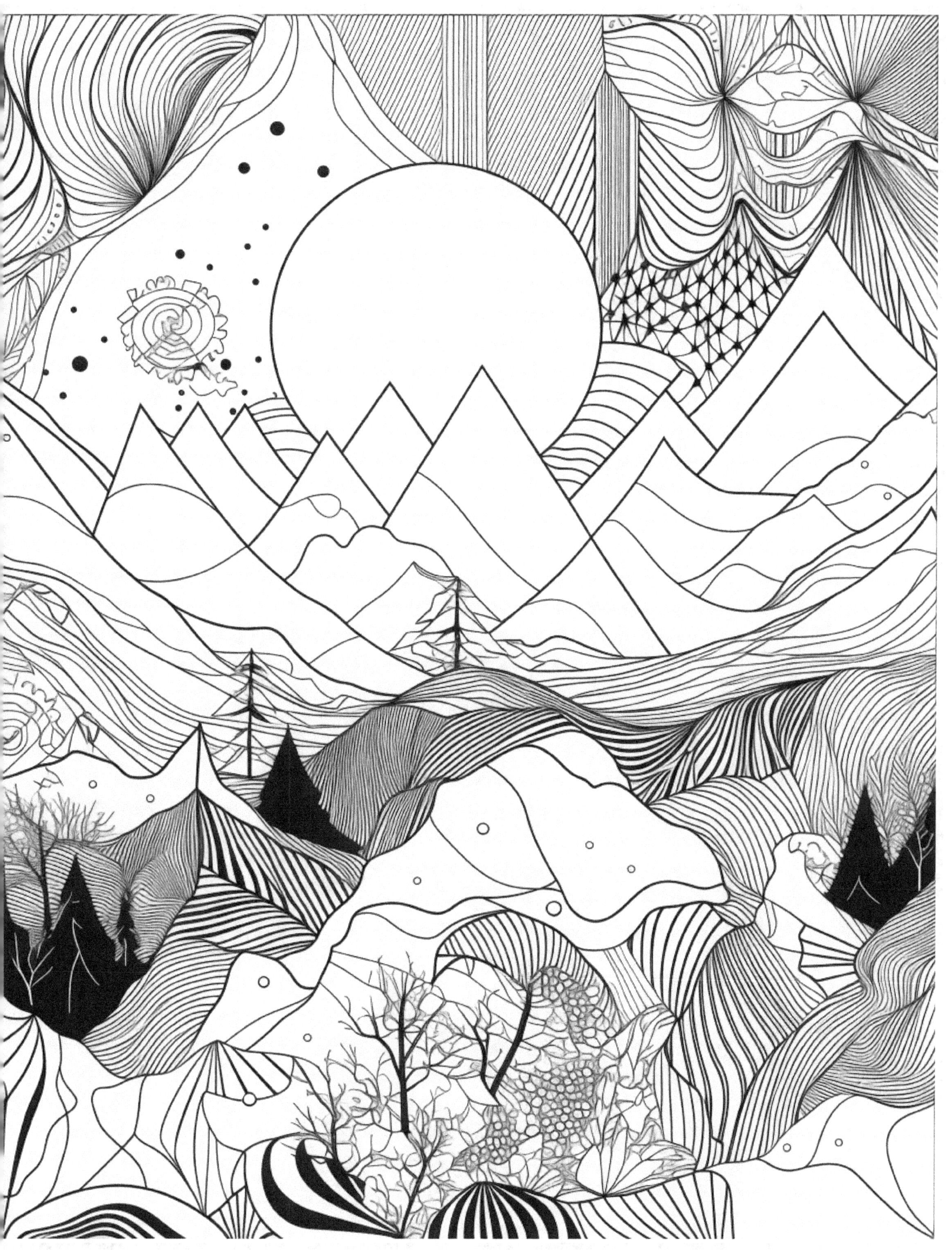

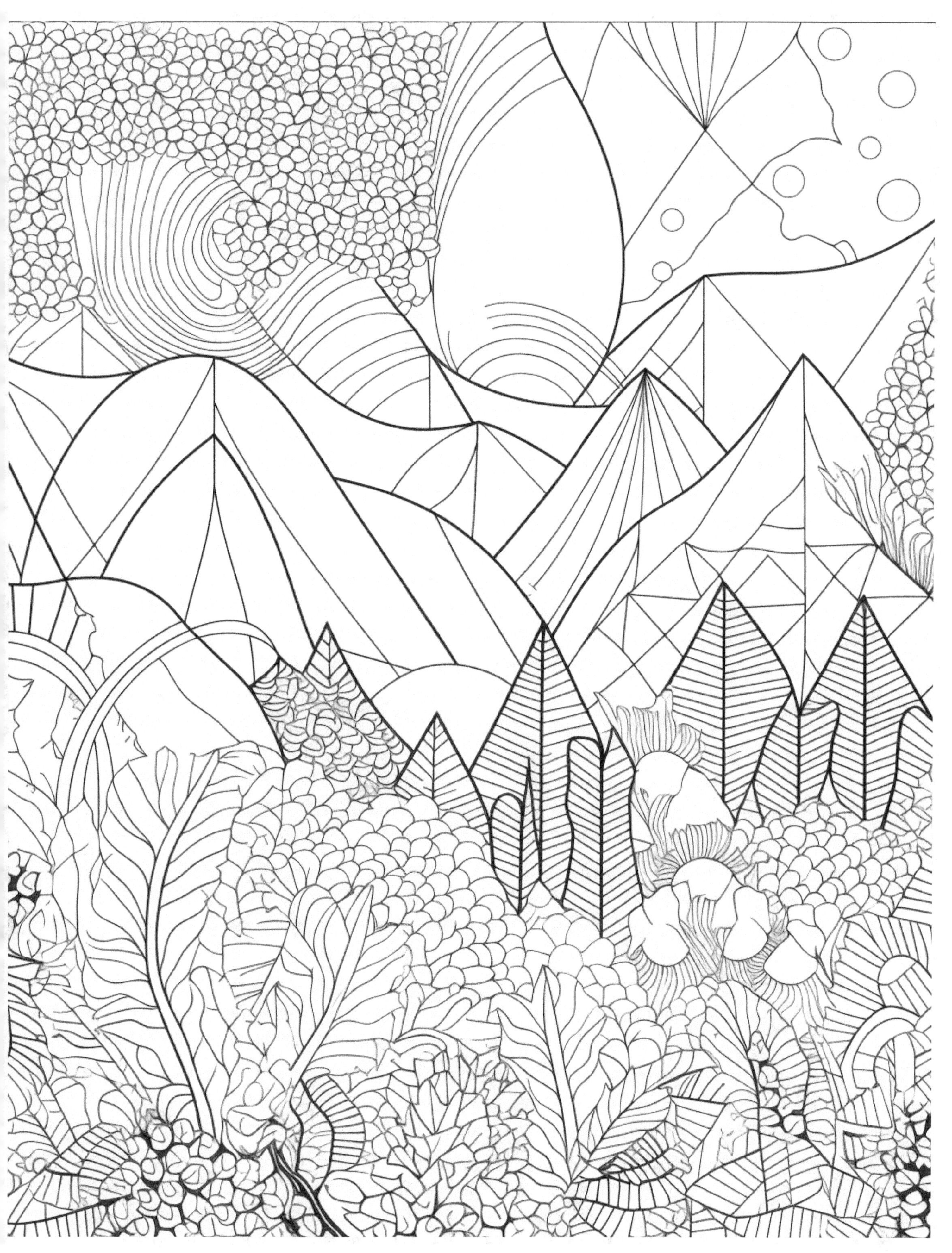

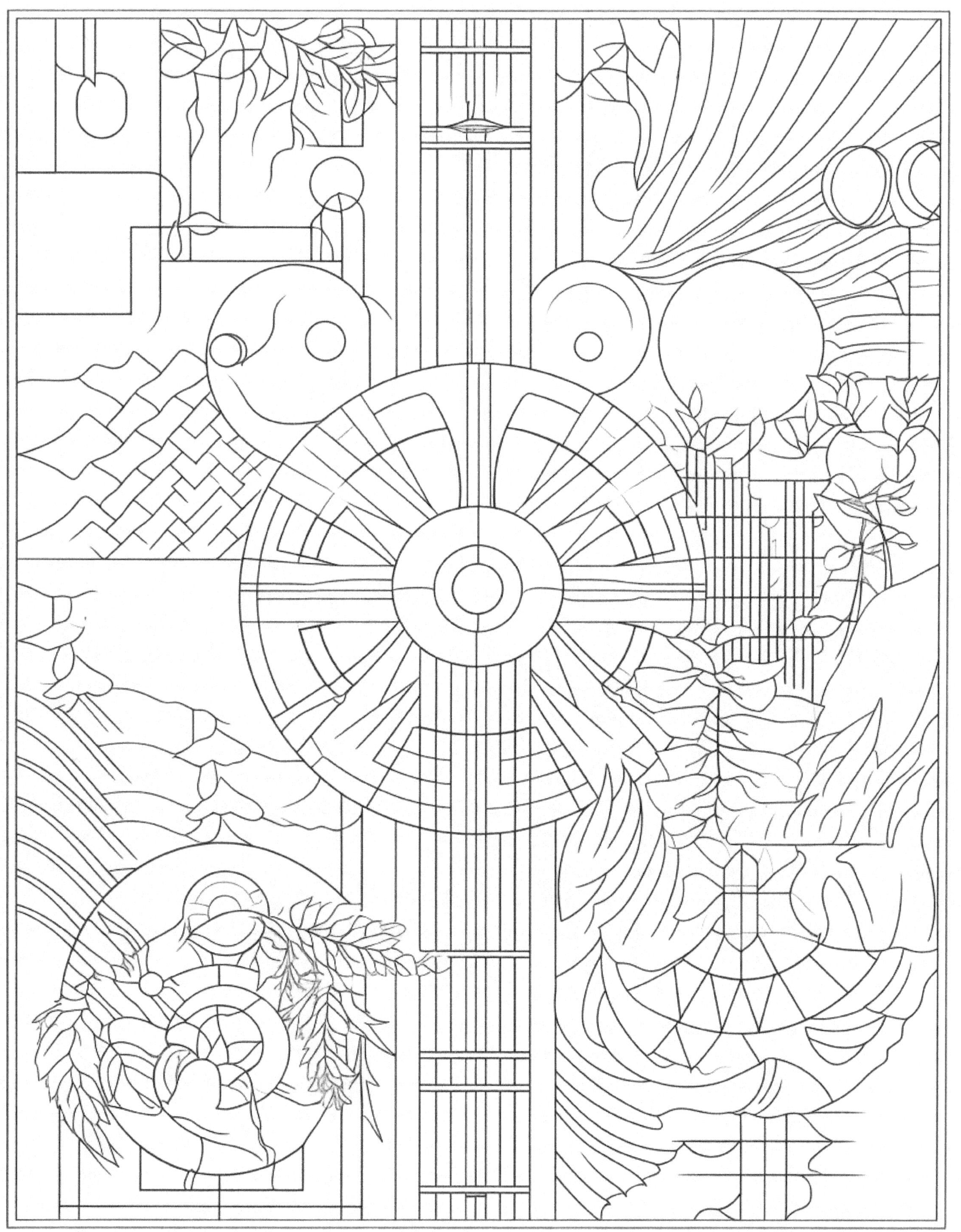

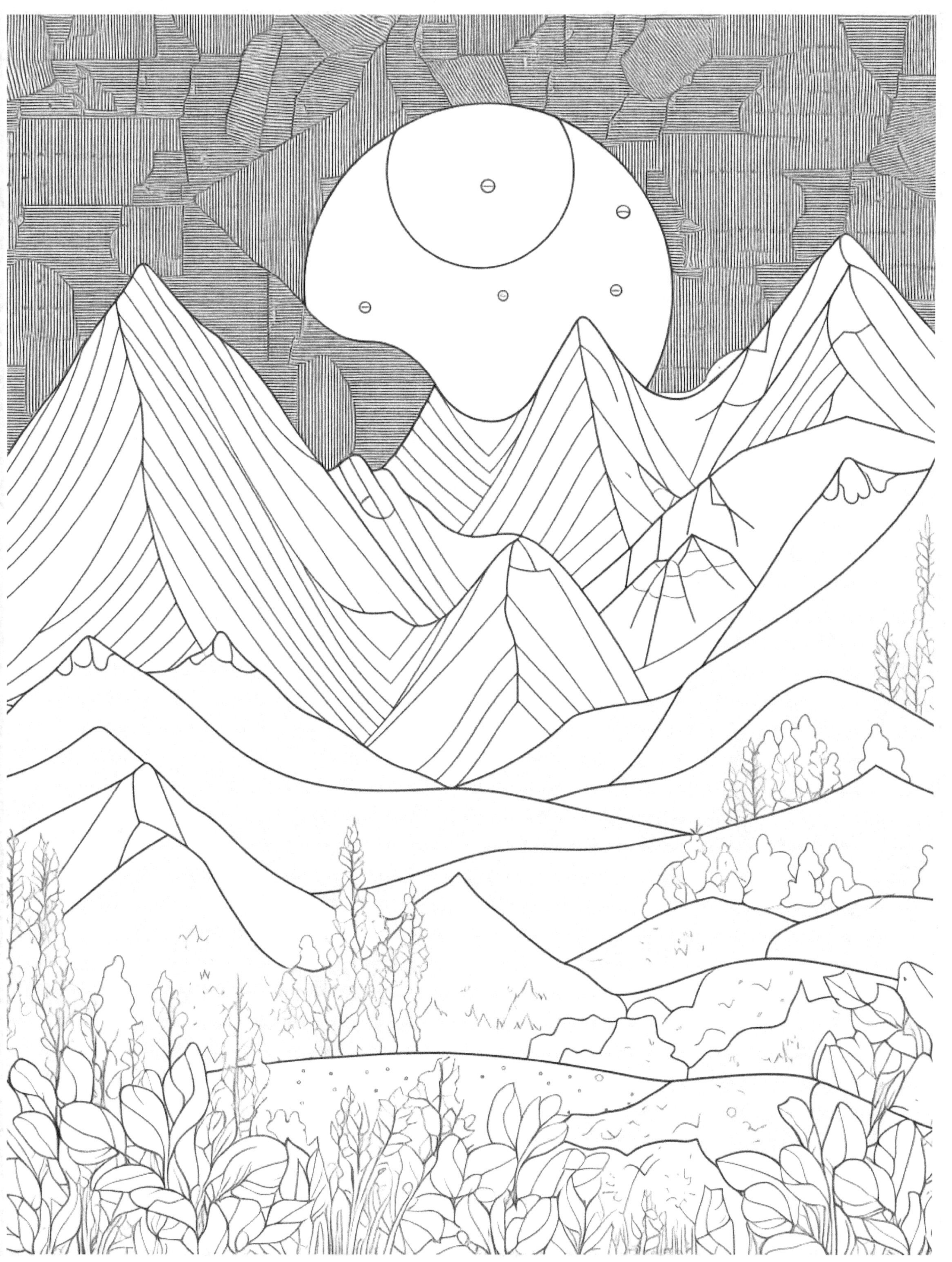

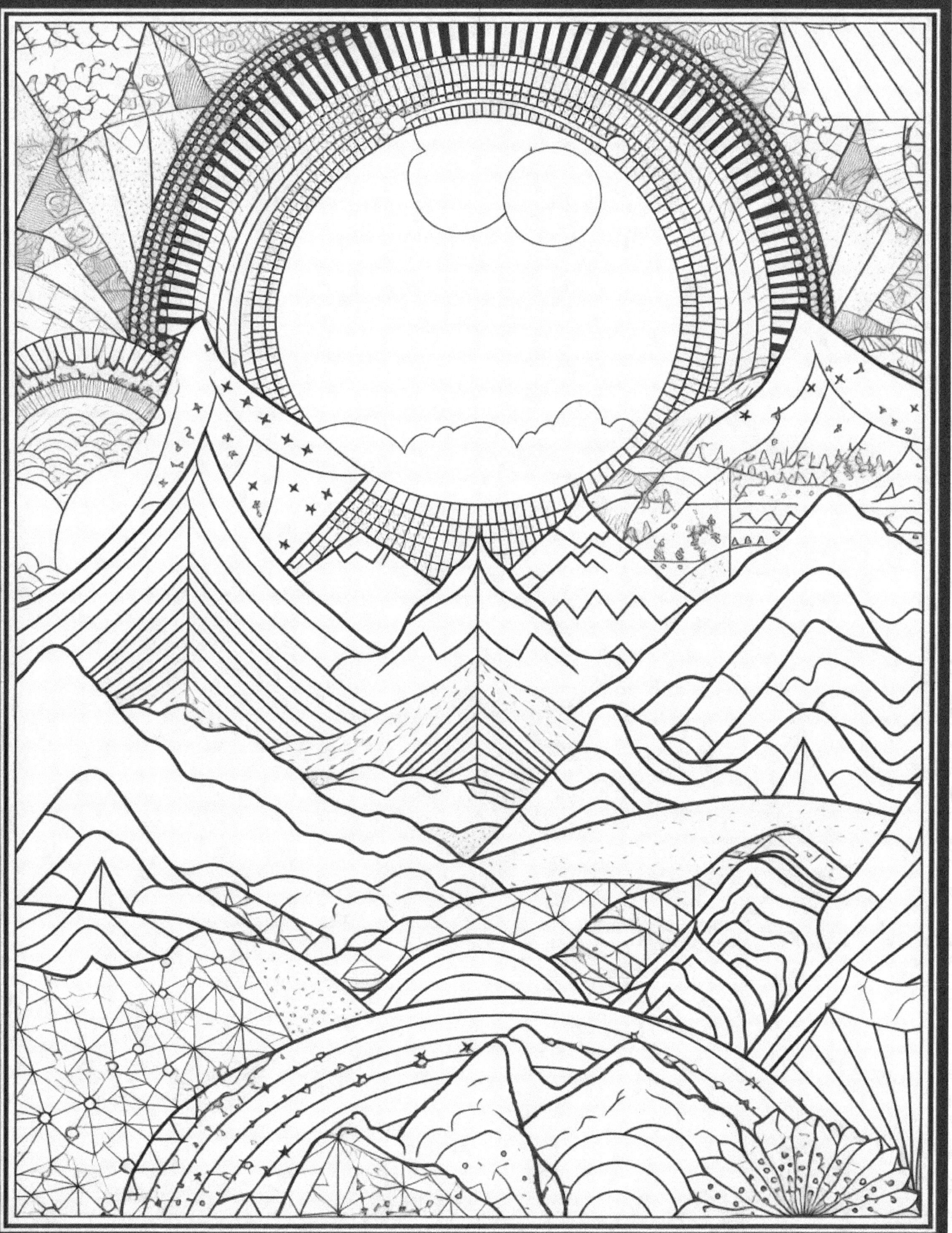

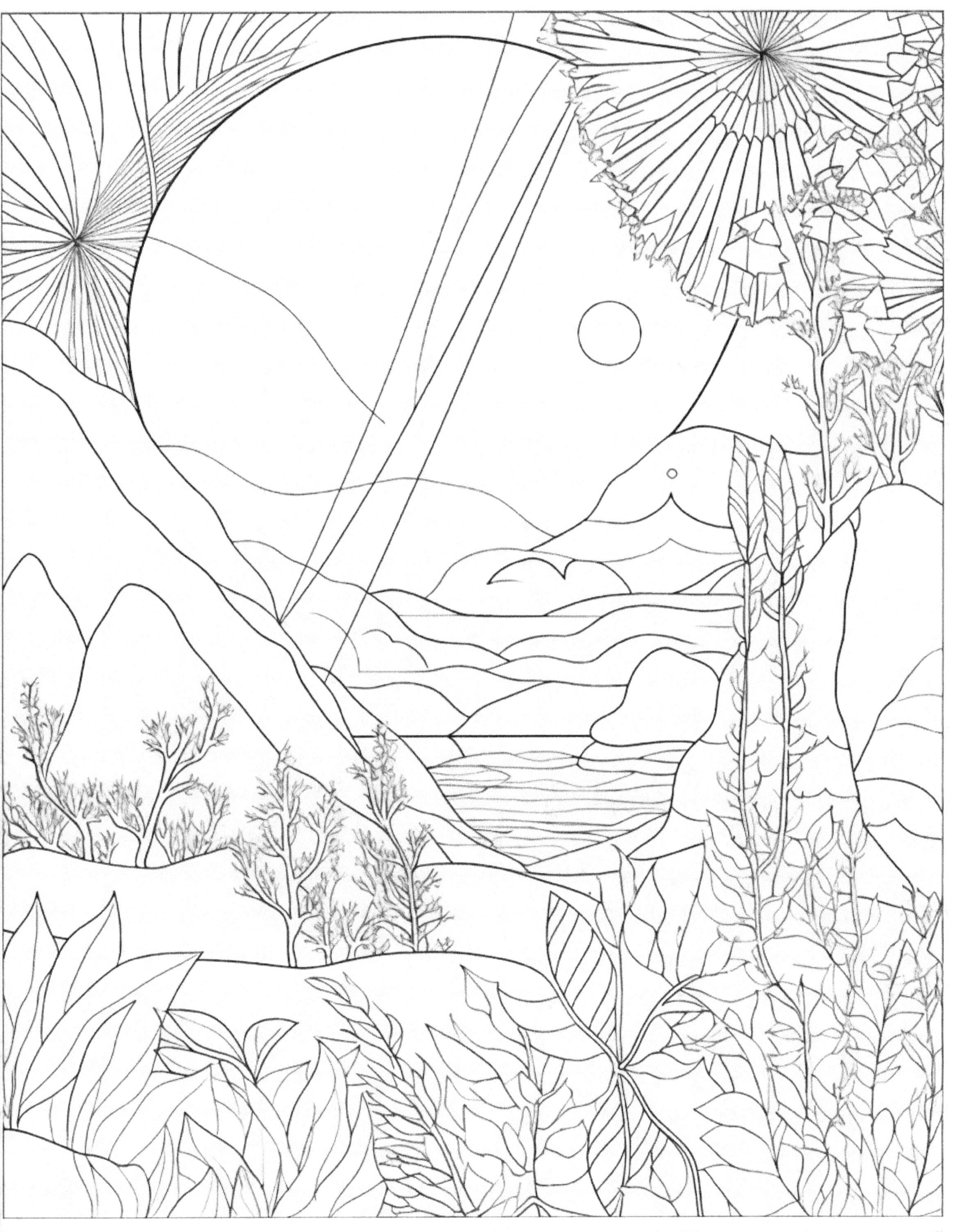

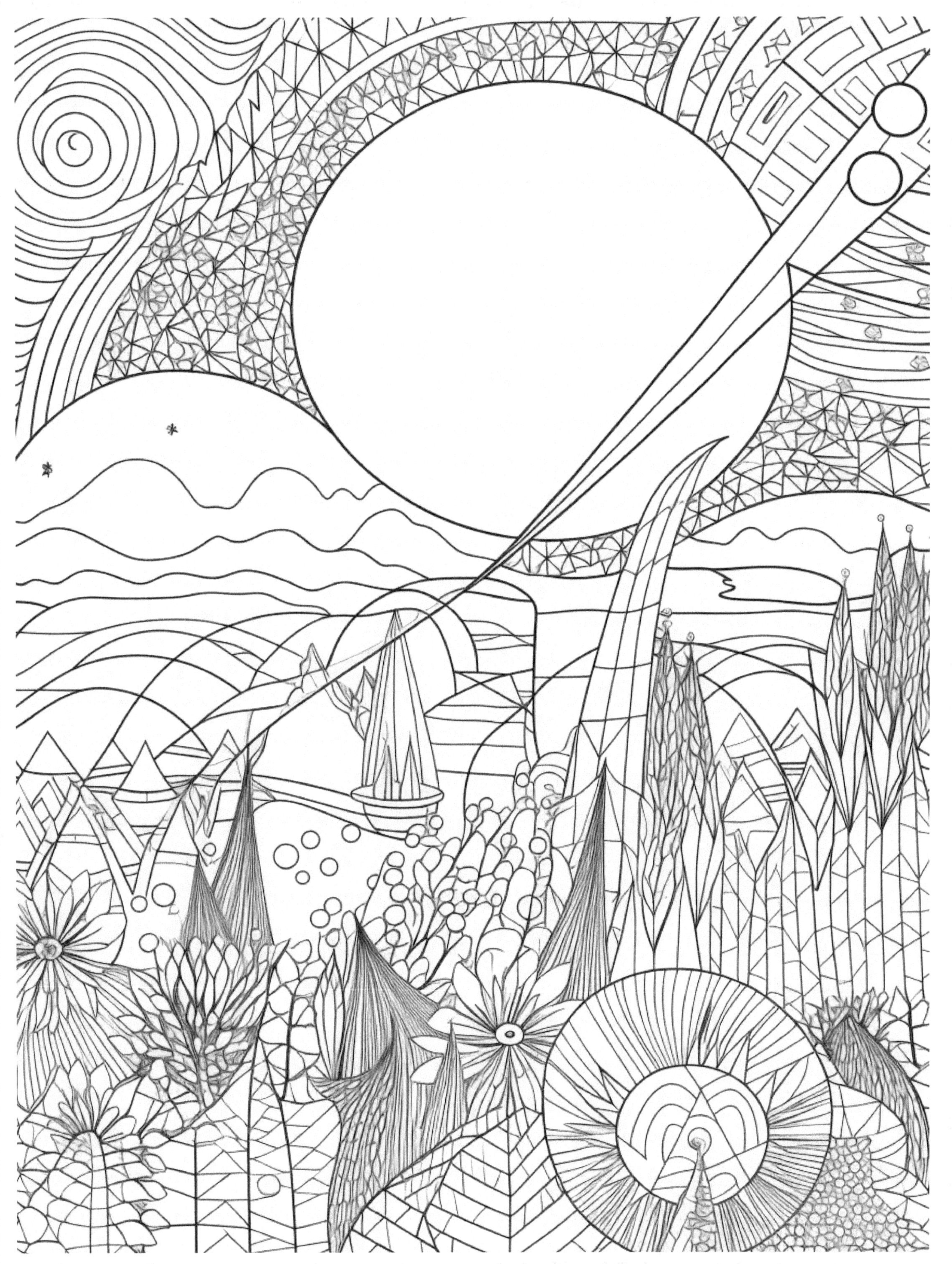

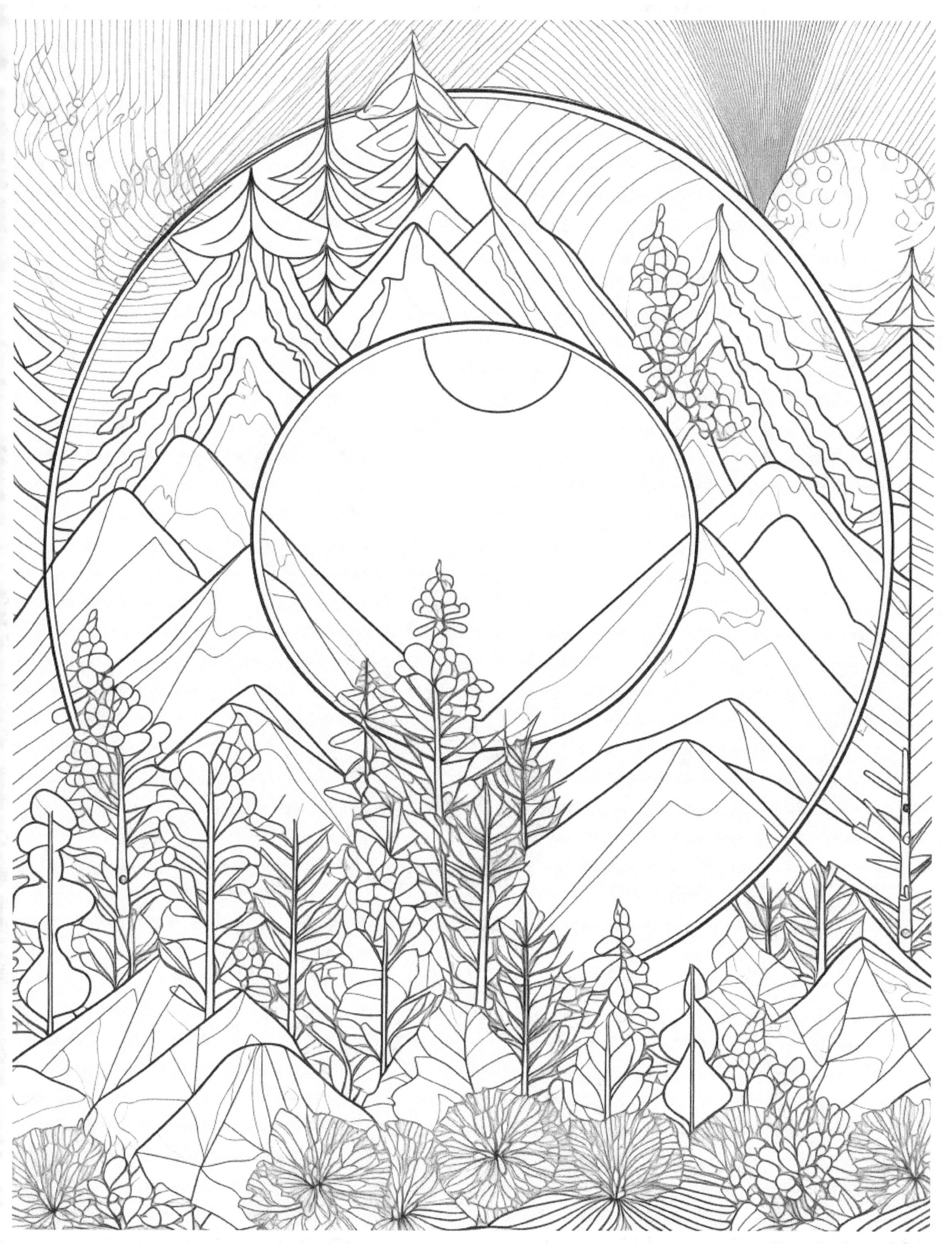

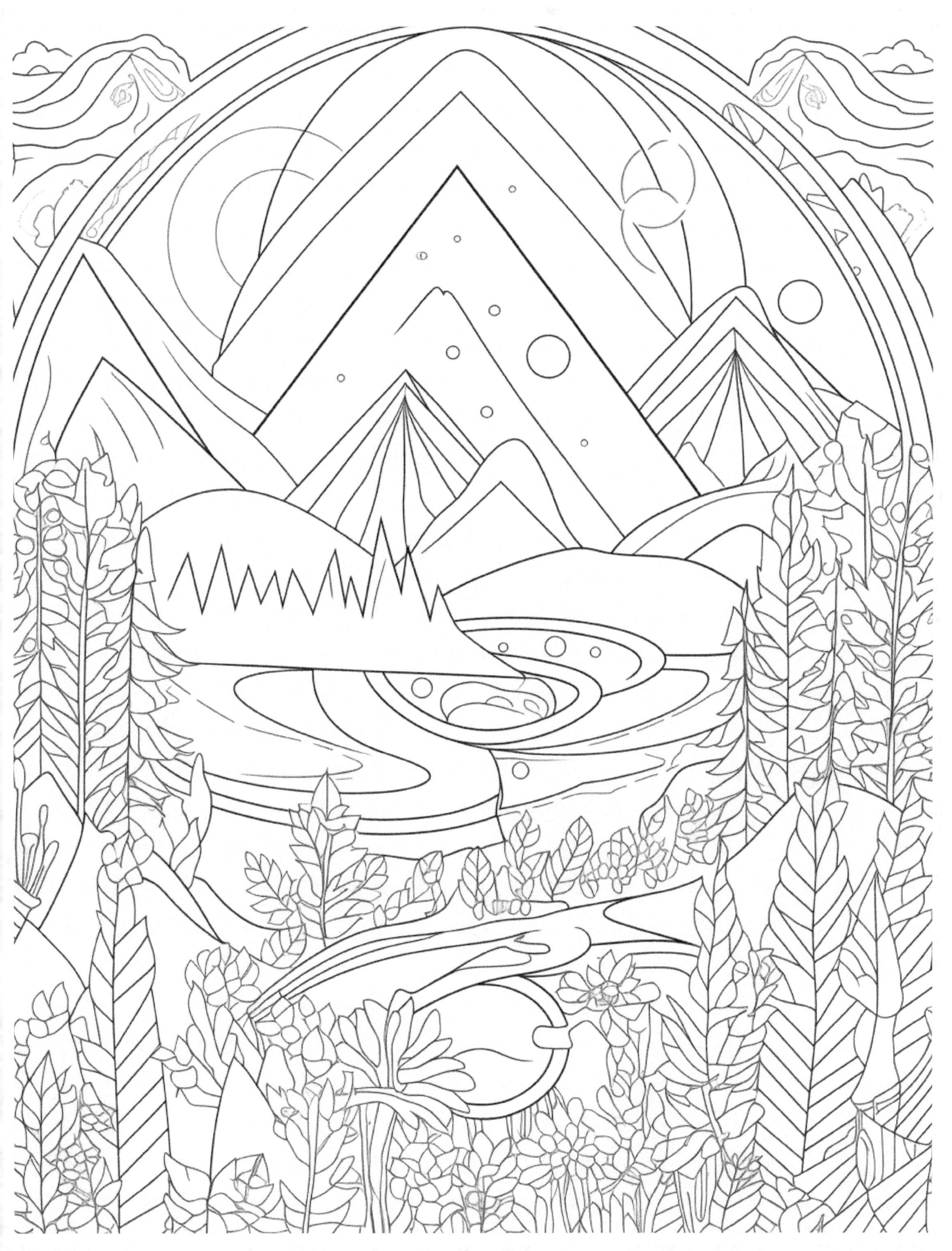

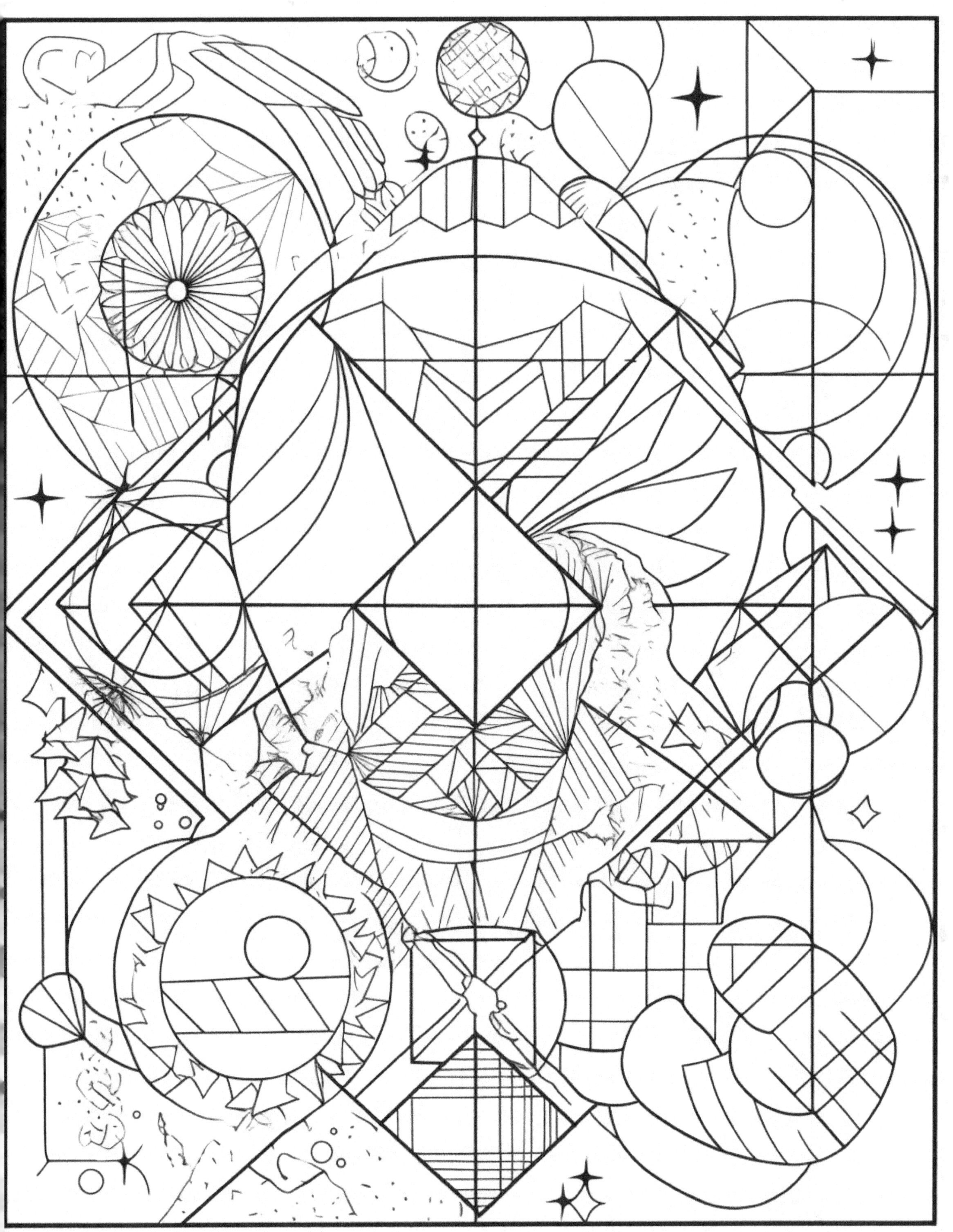

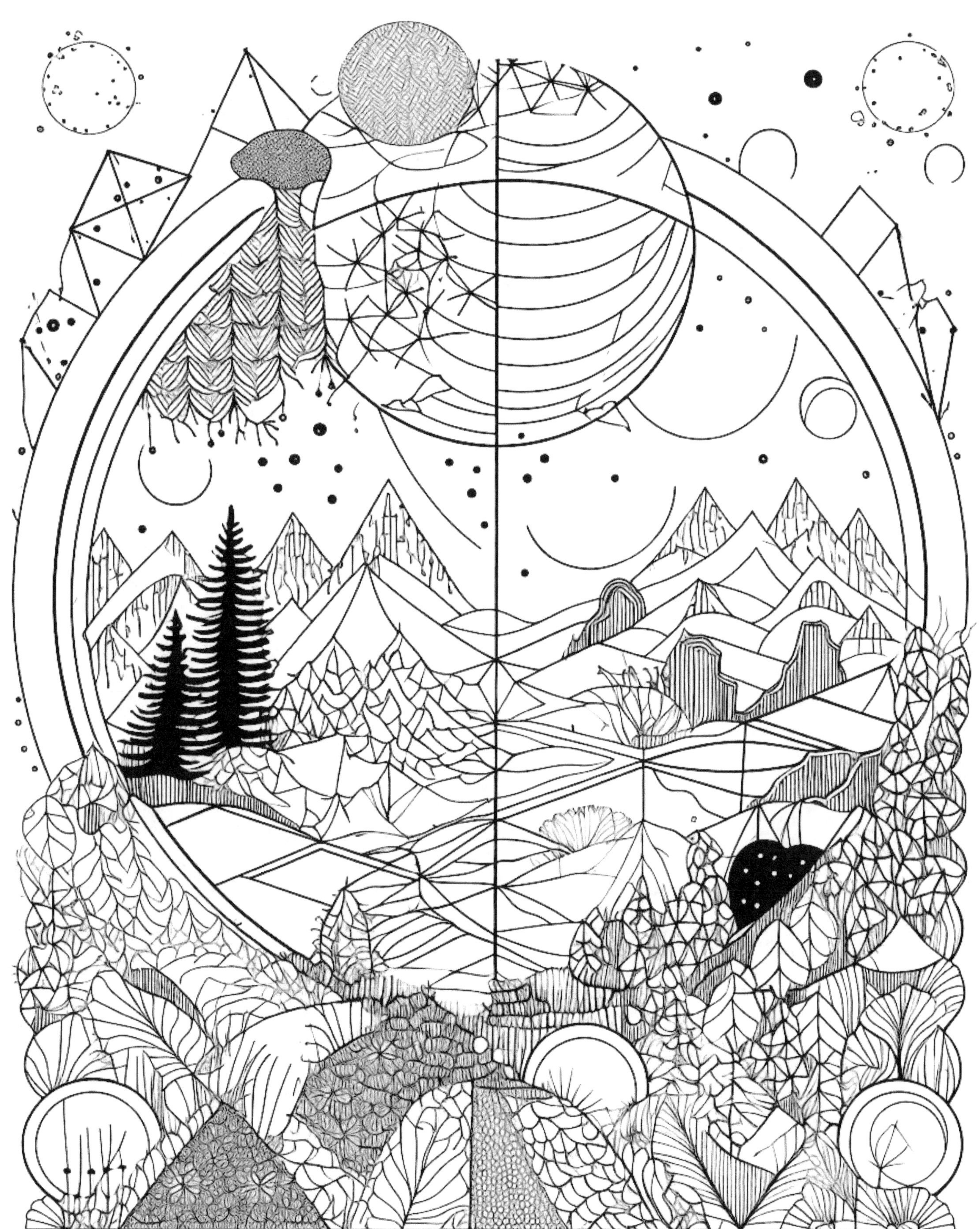

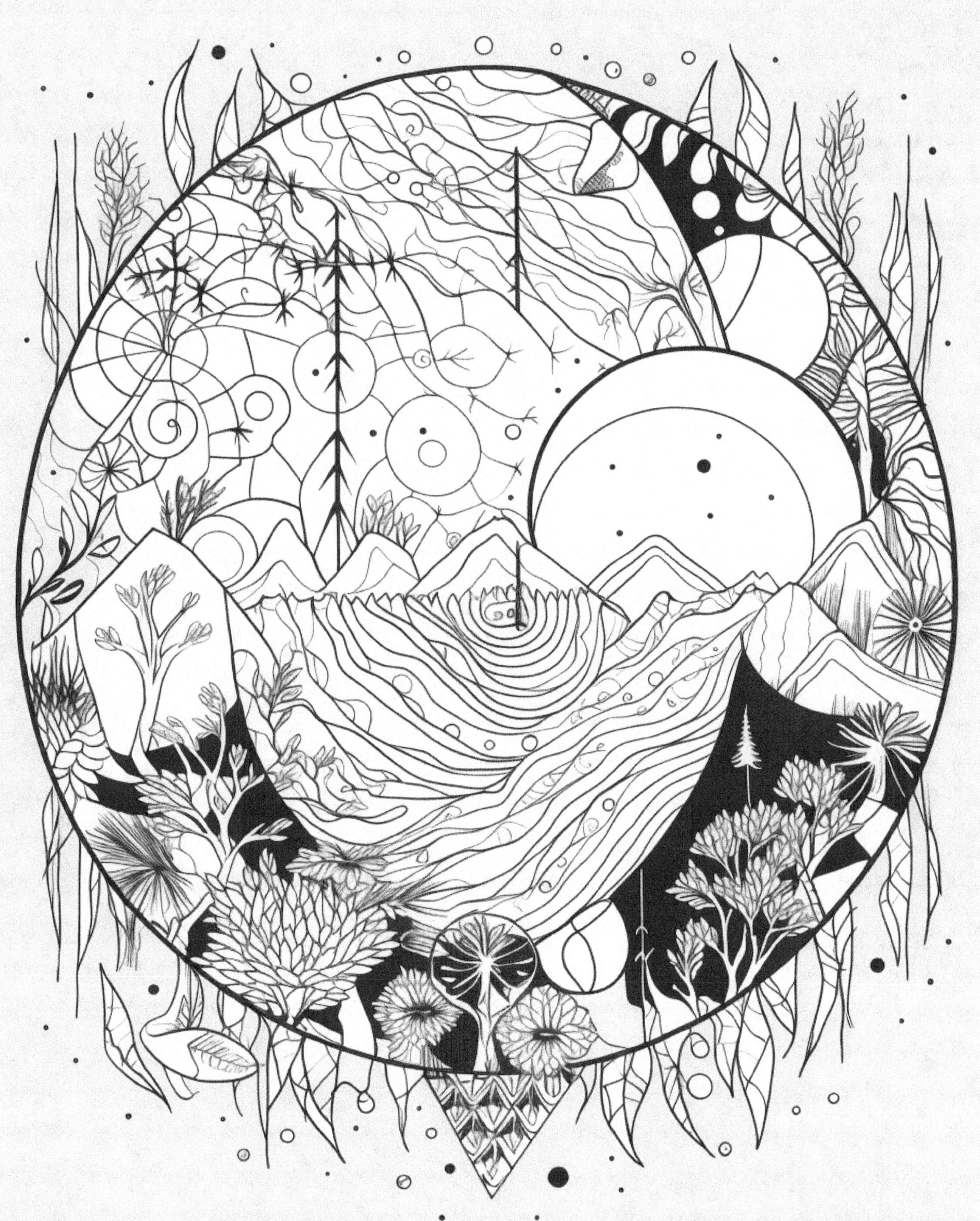

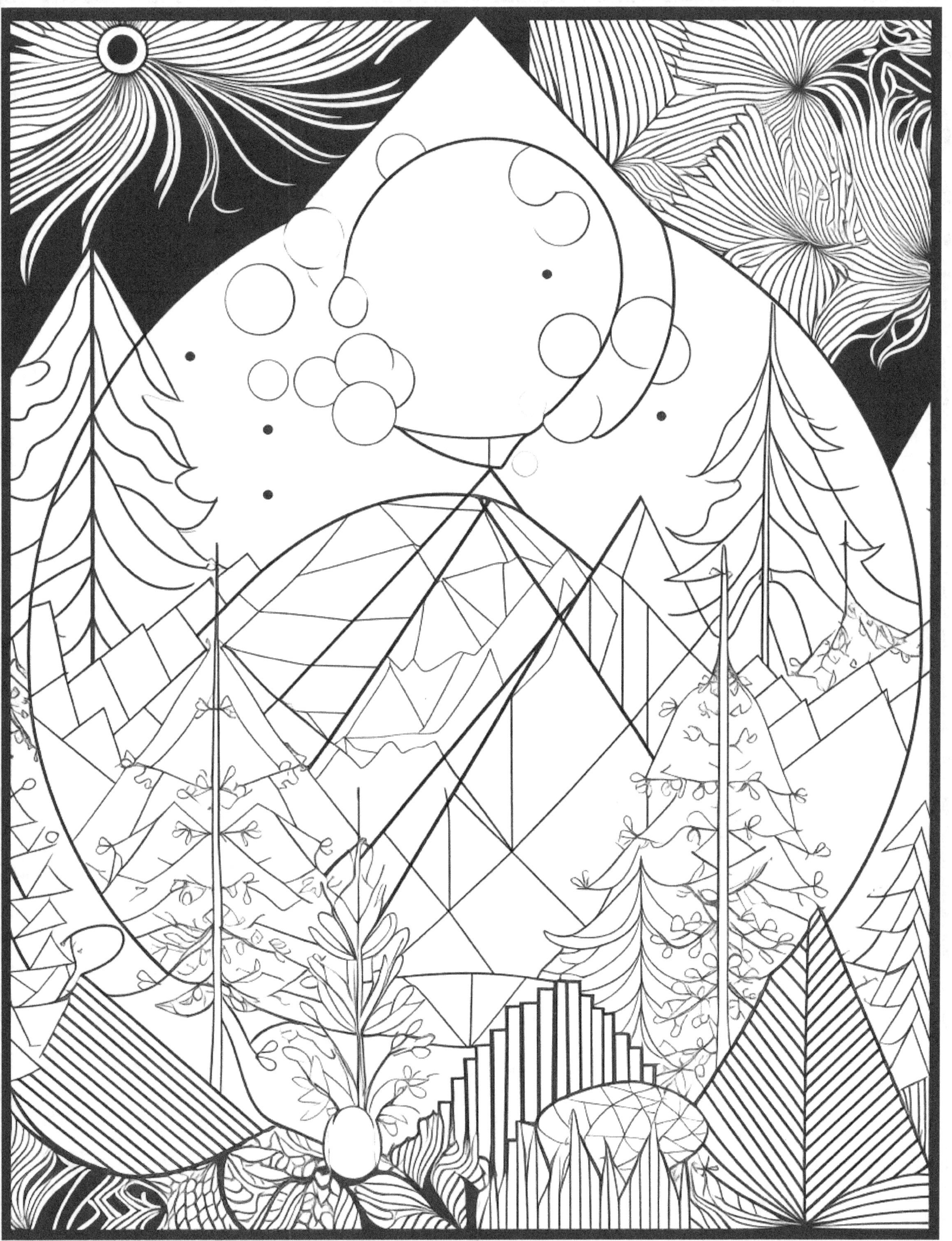

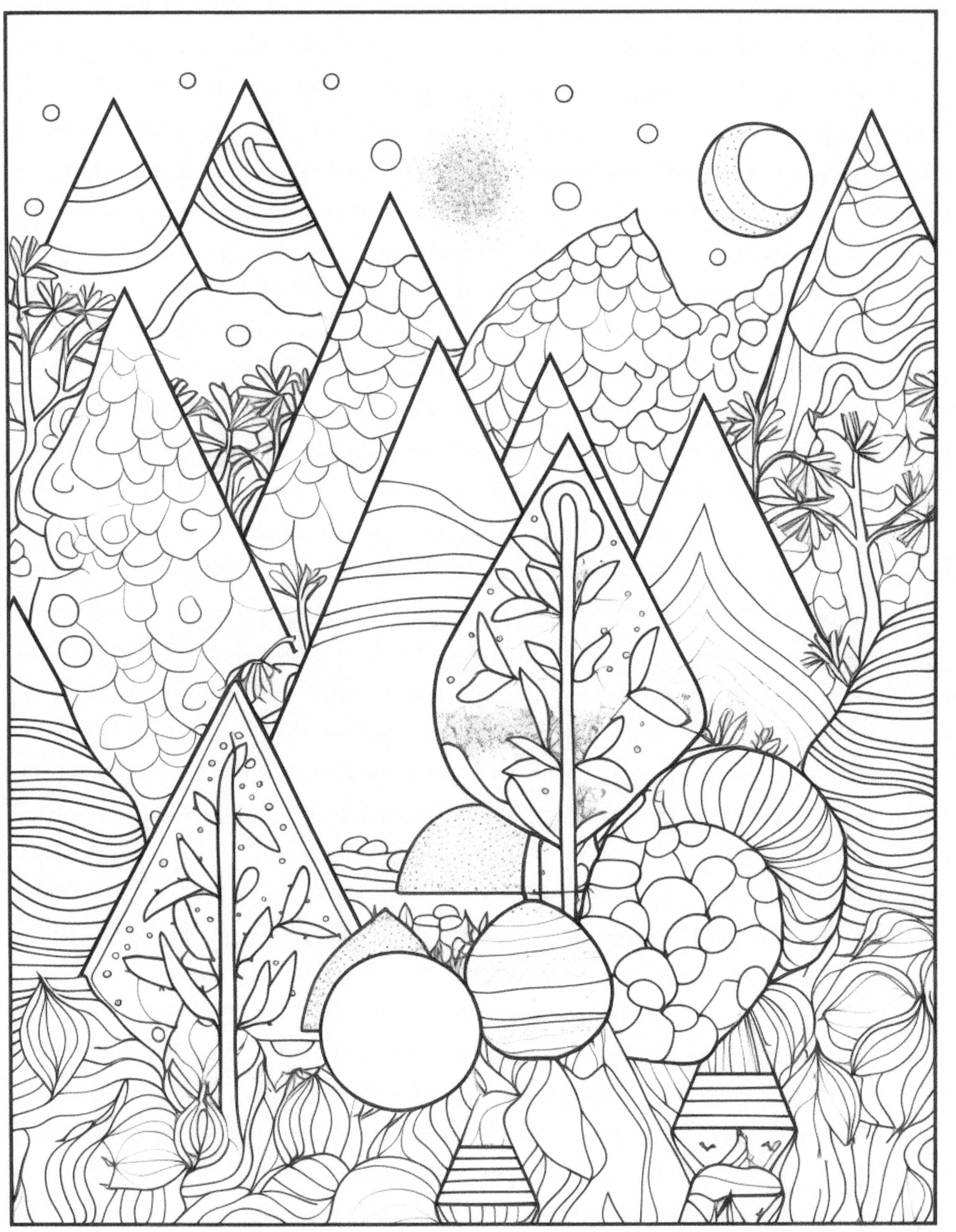

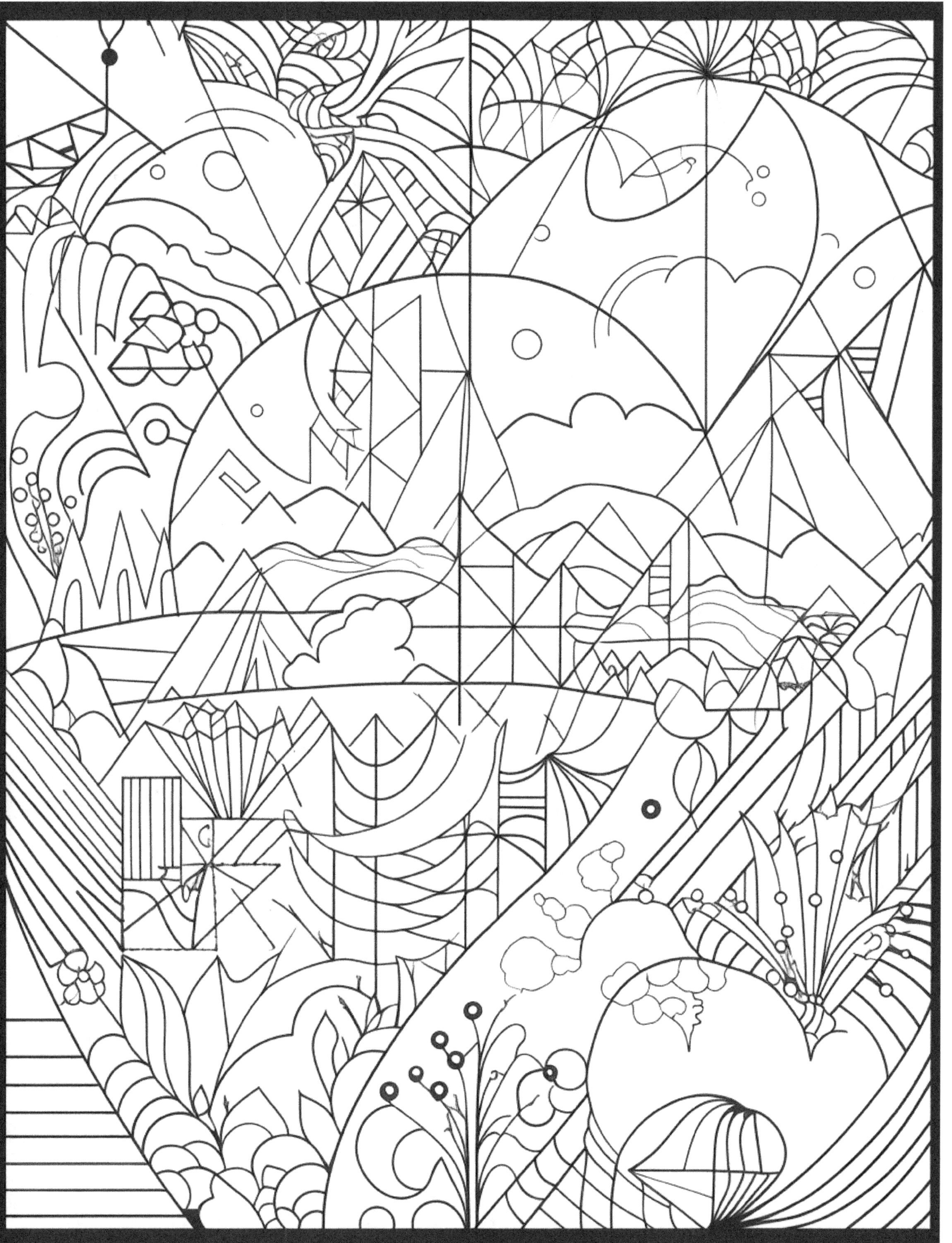

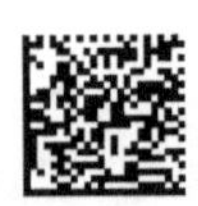

www.ingramcontent.com/pod-product-compliance
Lightning Source LLC
Chambersburg PA
CBHW081455250726
48662CB00009B/3095